CURES TH

OF JOSEMARÍA ESCRIVÁ

CURES

THROUGH THE INTERCESSION

OF JOSEMARÍA ESCRIVÁ

FLAVIO CAPUCCI

Scepter Publishers
Midwest Theological Forum

CURES THROUGH THE INTERCESSION OF JOSEMARÍA ESCRIVÁ

Originally published under the title *Un Mondo di Miracoli*
English translation published 2002 by Scepter Publishers, Inc.

Scepter Publishers, Inc.
P.O. Box 211, New York, N.Y. 10018
www.scepterpublishers.org

ISBN 0–889334–71–5

Composed in ITC Cheltenham Book

Printed in the United States of America

Contents

Preface

Blessed Josemaría Escrivá, the founder of Opus Dei, was born in Spain in 1902 and died in Rome in 1975. Even during his lifetime, he was widely regarded as someone extraordinarily close to God. After his death, many people all over the world began spontaneously praying for his intercession for all kinds of needs, large and small. A little card with a prayer for private devotion was quickly distributed for that purpose. In 1992, seventeen years after his death, he was declared Blessed. On October 6, 2002, Pope John Paul II will canonize him, numbering him among the saints—in large part because of miracles attributed to his intercession.

Msgr. Flavio Capucci has worked for many years to collect evidence for the cause, as head of an office Opus Dei set up for that purpose. In this book his office is referred to as "the Postulation." From the information he had amassed by 1996, Msgr. Capucci selected eighteen examples of favors obtained through Blessed Josemaría's intercession, both before and after his beatification, to be published in book form.

All of these are medical cures, for the simple reason that they admit of scientific proof and therefore can more readily be documented, as compared with the more numerous spiritual favors that people have reported. Capucci writes, "Among the favors Blessed Josemaría has obtained from God, there are many more spiritual ones than medical cures. But it is more difficult to assess the objectivity of the spiritual favors. Only medical instruments and techniques such as X-rays, clinical analyses, and reports can provide the indisputable data for verifying facts that have no scientific explanation."

The favors reported in this book are presented not only to show the effectiveness of Blessed Josemaría's intercession, but also to strengthen the reader's faith in the loving power of God, our Father, who always hears the prayers of his children and grants what is best for them. The author emphasizes in each account the spiritual dimension along with the physical and seeks to help us realize that, facts aside, God's ways remain mysterious. A clear example is provided in chapter 16. Rosa L. was cured of a life-threatening disorder of the pancreas, only to die of a heart attack not quite two years later.

Every account helps the reader to reflect on the deeper dimensions of God's care for us and the efficacy of our prayers when they spring from authentic faith.

Introduction

This is a book of extraordinary cures attributed to the intercession of Blessed Josemaría Escrivá. Such a book might seem odd to those who knew him personally, as well as those who have come to know him through his writings, for in his lifetime the founder of Opus Dei heralded the ordinary life of everyone's daily work, the normal and commonplace things that are so familiar to us. As for extraordinary things like miraculous cures, he used to say, "I don't need any miracles; there are more than enough for me in the Gospel. But I do want to see you fulfill your duty and cooperate with grace."[1]

Blessed Josemaría shunned the spectacular and ostentatious. He preferred what he termed the "heroism" of normal, ordinary things done well: "Have no doubt about this, you men and women in the world: Any evasion of the honest realities of daily life would be opposed to God's will for you."[2] It is significant that *The Way*, his best known book, contains a chapter on "Little Things," in addition to the chapters on classical themes of spirituality such as "Prayer," "Penance," and "Faith."

Nevertheless, the fact is well established that as soon as Blessed Josemaría left this world he began a new career as advocate in heaven. These pages relate some of the many extraordinary favors he has obtained for his numerous clients on earth. They include eighteen cures declared by medical experts to be without scientific explanation. The first, tenth, and last of these have been examined by Church authorities; the first cure and the last one have been officially declared miraculous by the Congregation for the Causes of Saints.

It is important to emphasize that these are all medical cures. Among the favors Blessed Josemaría has obtained from God, there are many more spiritual ones than medical cures. But it is more difficult to assess the objectivity of the spiritual favors. Only medical instruments and techniques such as X-

[1] *The Way*, no. 362.

[2] *Conversations with Monsignor Escrivá de Balaguer*, no. 114.

favors. Only medical instruments and techniques such as X-rays, clinical analyses, and reports can provide the indisputable data for verifying facts that have no scientific explanation. This is why the miracles supporting causes of canonization nearly always have to do with medicine. This volume includes only such extraordinary cures.

A brief summary of each cure will be presented in accurate but non-technical language so that anyone can understand it. Except for cases that are already publicly known, fictitious names are used, out of respect for the privacy of people concerned. This accords with the normal practice of specialized journals when they discuss clinical cases.

The principal significance of the stories told in these pages concerns the actual lives of persons dramatically changed by divine intervention, for a genuine miracle objectively transcends the laws of nature and can therefore be caused only by God. It follows that a miracle manifests God's presence and action in time. But speaking theologically, a miracle also signifies and aids our salvation, for it witnesses to the divinity of Christ, in whom God's manifestation reaches its culmination. It offers tangible proof that God is merciful Love and, at the same time, supports our belief in a Word which is not simply an announcement of truth but also a life-giving reality.

The Gospel relates numerous miracles Jesus performed for all kinds of people, from beggars and lepers to centurions and synagogue officials. What these people had in common was an honest simplicity that allowed them to be transformed by faith. Other characters we meet in the Gospel were closed to divine grace; in their disbelief they were unable to ask Jesus for help and could only dispute with him.

The stories in this book can help readers increase their resolve to live more consistently as Christians, with an optimism founded not on wishful thinking, but on factual evidence. While some among us are so busy deploring the moral degradation of the world that they can see no signs of hope, many others are moved by the same evils to pray for deliverance and forgiveness. Evidently God listens to their prayers, for our world continues to witness miracles.

It is easier to fight when victory is assured by a faith that unites the extraordinary with the natural. This helps to explain the paradox of extraordinary cures attributed to an ordinary priest, Blessed Josemaría Escrivá. His high degree of sanctity coexists with a very human claim that he was "not one for miracles." [3] Yet he also encouraged everyone to have great faith in God, so as to acquire "that familiarity and confidence which prompts us to ask him, like children, for the moon!" [4]

[3] See *The Way*, no. 583
[4] *Christ Is Passing By*, no. 64.

1. A Tumor the Size of an Orange

"The instantaneous, complete, and permanent cure of multiple tumoral masses (atypical lipomatose tumor)." (June 1976)[5]

The cure of Sister Concepción Boullón Rubio, a Carmelite Sister of Charity, took place in June 1976 near Madrid, Spain. This cure is of particular importance because, after a detailed and rigorous study, its miraculous nature was recognized by the Congregation for the Causes of Saints, the Church body with authority in these matters. This enabled the beatification process of the founder of Opus Dei to proceed to its conclusion on May 17, 1992, in St. Peter's Square.

On November 6, 1981, the Congregation formally authorized the inquiry *super miro* (of the possible miracle) to begin in accord with its procedures. On November 16 the Congregation sent instructions and questionnaires to the Archbishop of Madrid, Cardinal Vicente Enrique y Tarancón, for examination of the witnesses. On December 18, he issued a decree establishing a board of examiners. During the process, which lasted from January 21 to April 3, 1982, ten witnesses testified: the person cured, the two doctors involved in the case and another doctor who examined her after the cure, three nuns who lived in the convent with Sister Concepción (the Superior and two others who had followed closely her illness and cure), and three of her relatives (two sisters and a niece).

The Congregation issued a decree confirming the validity of the procedure on November 20, 1984. As the examination of the life and virtues of the Servant of God, Josemaría Escrivá, was still under way, the documentation concerning the miracle was deposited in the Congregation's archives.

Once the heroic virtues were recognized (by pontifical decree on April 9, 1990), the relevant committees of the Congregation began formal examination of the miracle. The Medical

[5] The *Positio super miraculo*, documenting this extraordinary cure, is contained in a 410-page book that includes the statements of witnesses, the medical reports, and all the proofs required to demonstrate the miracle.

Committee met on June 30, 1990, and the Theological Consultors on July 14. Both bodies gave a unanimously favorable judgment. The doctors declared that the instantaneous, complete, and permanent cure of Sister Concepción had no natural explanation, and the theologians concluded that this was attributable to the intercession of the founder of Opus Dei.

The pontifical decree acknowledging the miracle came on July 6, 1991, and in September the Holy Father set the date of the beatification for May 17, 1992. On that day the founder of Opus Dei was declared to be among God's blessed in heaven in a solemn ceremony before some three hundred thousand persons who gathered in St. Peter's Square from all over the world.

Two infirmities

Sister Concepción Boullón was born in the province of Teruel, Spain, on January 23, 1906. At age twenty-three she discerned her vocation to religious life and entered the Congregation of the Carmelites of Charity. At the time of her cure she was seventy years old and resided in the community's convent at San Lorenzo de El Escorial, near Madrid.

Her clinical record prior to the tumors mentioned only rheumatic discomfort and obesity, for which she had received occasional treatment. In 1972 Sister Concepción began to experience gastric symptoms, anemia, weight loss, and asthenia. Two years later, some tumorous and very painful lumps appeared on her left shoulder, on the top of her left foot, and on her right thumb. These gradually increased in size, reaching their largest growth early in 1975.

As described by Dr. José W., the community's physician, a radiological study carried out around that time showed "in the shoulder an extra-osseous tumor surrounding the head of the humerus, with areas of greater density, calcified, the size of an orange, which in our opinion was replacing the capsule and soft parts of the joint. There was a similar tumor a little smaller than a hazelnut on the distal third of the thumb, with some areas of calcification. On the foot several lesions appeared on the dorsum, which appeared to have replaced the soft parts of the different joints of the foot. These were somewhere between the size of a hazelnut and an almond."

This combination of symptoms ordinarily called for a biopsy to determine the nature of the tumors and whether or not they were malignant. But, as the doctor continued, "The patient's general condition was so poor . . . that we were unable to do so; I feared that any operation on a shoulder so badly inflamed, even if it were only for the purposes of extracting the minimum tissue necessary for histological analysis, could produce hemorrhaging which the patient was not in a condition to bear." Treatment was therefore limited to painkillers.

While these tumors were developing, gastric disorders from which Sister Concepción had suffered since 1972 worsened. X-rays carried out at the beginning of 1975 showed a gastric ulcer and a hiatus hernia, in addition to biliary lithiasis. The conjuncture of these two conditions caused her condition to deteriorate rapidly.

One of the nuns, Sister María del Pilar, reported that "these lumps became so painful that she had to incline her head to one side, because of the pain they caused when she held it in the normal position. . . . She became much worse, her voice grew very weak, and she spent almost the whole day sitting in an armchair with many cushions." The pains grew so intense that she could hardly sleep. She also began to suffer melenas (hemorrhages in the digestive system), which caused severe anemia. In a few months her weight rapidly declined to about ninety pounds. According to the Sister Superior, "at the worst stage of the illness, Sister Concepción looked like a corpse."

The sudden cure

By the spring of 1976, Sister Concepción's condition had reached its terminal phase. This was apparent to the other nuns and confirmed by the physician's comments. Sister María del Pilar recalls, "When the Superior told him that Sister Concepción sometimes ate something she shouldn't, the doctor replied: 'Let her be, poor thing, she has very little time left.' "

The Superior related that the doctor once told her "not to bother Sister, since she would not be with us much longer.

Because she had such a serious illness, . . . and lumps were appearing everywhere, we feared the worst. . . . Her face took on an earthen color. . . . We all thought that Sister Concepción was dying, and her sister Pilar thought so, too."

The physician himself put it this way: "Our view was that she could die of this illness. I reported that prognosis to the Superior and the nuns who were looking after the patient. This was based on the fact that her general condition was steadily worsening, the digestive pathology was following an alarming course, and the tumors were causing a great deal of pain and general wasting (cachexia)."

The radiologist was of the same opinion. In March 1976 he was asked to take an X-ray of the abdomen and later to complete the radiological exploration in search of a possible gastric tumor that, it was thought at the time, might be causing all of the symptoms. In his words: "I wanted to make it clear that I performed no further explorations because the patient was in such a serious condition; I even felt troubled over the ones I had done because they increased her suffering so greatly. . . . Moreover, I knew that the gastroenterologist and the other doctors thought that we were dealing with an irreversible tumoral process with metastasis."

As the weeks passed, Sister Concepción calmly prepared for death. She totally accepted her condition and abandoned herself trustingly into God's hands. This is clear from what she had said on several occasions, and others confirmed: at no time had she asked God for a cure. According to one of the nuns, "We in the Community did not feel that we ought to pray for her cure either, as Sister Concha's [Concepción's] serenity and acceptance of God's will edified us so much. . . . She had never prayed for a cure because she regarded her apparently imminent death with characteristic serenity and humility. In her view, it was all God's doing. After her extraordinary cure . . . she thought that if God had prolonged her life . . . it was so that she could go on serving him and attain greater holiness."

The patient, then, and the other nuns in her community, were calmly reconciled to the imminent prospect of death. But, as we shall see, that was not God's plan. He chose to glorify himself through his servant, Msgr. Josemaría Escrivá, by means of a miraculous cure.

This extraordinary event occurred in the space of a single night. It is described here in the words Sister Concepción herself used during the investigation: "I was cured of the tumors I have mentioned in June 1976. I cannot be more specific about the date. I remember that on the night I experienced the cure, I had felt some particular pains and a troublesome irritation on my left shoulder and foot. I did not notice [then] that some of the tumors had disappeared. I slept an hour or an hour and a half."

Sister Concepción had told one of the witnesses about the considerable discomfort she had experienced that night until about five in the morning. Then "she fell asleep, and at seven, when the community awoke, she went to take a shower, thinking that it might produce some relief."

Sister Concepción goes on: "I got up, and when I was in the shower, I noticed that I didn't have the lump on my left shoulder. I was rather puzzled by this, and went to look at my bed to see if there were any stains there; I didn't see anything. As I was getting dressed, when I put on my shoes I noticed that I didn't have any tumors on my left foot either. I quickly went to find the Superior, to tell her what was happening to me." When she heard that the lumps had disappeared, the Superior naturally thought that they had burst, but was told that there were no stains on the sheets.

That morning Sister Concepción was able to attend Mass with her community—something she had not been able to do for some time. In the final stage of her infirmity she had been unable to rise until eleven in the morning or even midday.

It is not surprising that no one recalled the exact date on which the cure took place. One of the nuns explained that the Sisters dedicate themselves entirely to God in complete detachment from their own health; this was particularly so in the case of Sister Concepción, as we have seen. Abandoning themselves into the hands of their Father, God, they lack clinical interest in their physical condition. When the tumors suddenly disappeared without leaving a trace, no one in the community thought of making it known. Even the attending physician learned of it only by chance some days later, when he went to Sunday Mass in the community's chapel. Sister Concepción relates that not until then did she inform him that the tumors had disappeared. "He told me to go to his clinic the next day, but it was a fortnight or over a month before I went."

Thanks to the testimony of some of the nuns, the cure can at least be dated to the middle of June 1976, for on the 20th or 21st of that month, the Superior had asked Sister Concepción to go with Sister María del Pilar, who was having some X-rays done. Sister Pilar states: "I was really surprised that the Superior told her to come with me, because I knew how ill she had been. But I could clearly see that she was walking without difficulty, and I could detect none of the previous signs of her illness; what struck me most was the difference that had come over her face—now she was lively and expressive."

Sister María del Pilar adds an important detail: When the radiologist saw Sister Concepción standing up straight, he was surprised, as he had taken X-rays of her a few months earlier and could personally vouch for her poor condition at that time. The following conversation, summarized by the nun in her declaration, took place between them:

"Sister, what has happened to you?"

"Well, doctor, I'm getting better, but I don't know why."

"If I were still a student I'd put this case under study, because it's one for the history books!"

Msgr. Josemaría Escrivá's role in the cure

While neither Sister Concepción nor the other nuns had prayed for the cure, her sisters Josefina and Felisa Boullón had asked God for it through the intercession of Opus Dei's founder. These two unmarried women lived in Montalbán, in the province of Teruel, and frequently spoke with their sister by telephone about the course of her illnesses. As they managed a pharmacy, they also regularly sent her the painkillers she needed.

Toward the end of 1975, they began to pray for their sister's recovery through the intercession of Msgr. Escrivá. As they explained it, their decision to do so had resulted from a magazine article attacking the founder of Opus Dei, who had died a few months earlier, and subsequent table conversation at Christmas, 1975. Felisa Boullón writes: "In spite of not really liking Opus Dei all that much, it seemed to me that those criticisms were unjust and biased. My reaction was to implore the Blessed Virgin—since the Servant of God had had great devotion to her—to make clear the truth about this son of hers. Then I prayed to her through the mediation of the Servant of God for my sister, as well as for other intentions which I don't remember."

From then on Felisa prayed very often for her sister's cure through Msgr. Escrivá's intercession. "We wanted the truth about Msgr. Josemaría Escrivá to be known," says Sister Concepción's other sister, Josefina. "It hurt us to hear the things that were said about him. In the prayers I offered for my sister I asked that, if possible, she would recover her health, and if not, that she would die a good death. I said these prayers nearly every morning while busy with housework."

One day, while travelling by car with a third sister, they prayed the Rosary for Sister Concepción's health and for a niece of theirs, through the intercession of Msgr. Escrivá. Felisa mentions another noteworthy point: "That day, a cousin had given me a book and some prayer cards of the Servant of God. This took place toward the end of June [1976]. From then on, whenever we said the Rosary together as a family, we offered it for my sister, through the intercession of the Servant of God."

As this statement shows, it was precisely around the time that the sisters increased their prayers that the cure took place. It was much later, however, before they learned that their prayers had been answered. It happened very naturally. One day, as they used to do from time to time, they telephoned Sister Concepción at El Escorial. Josefina Boullón described the conversation as follows:

> On one occasion when I spoke to her by telephone I noticed that her voice was normal. I asked her what had happened

to make her voice sound so much better. She answered, "I'm very well. The lumps on my shoulder and foot have disappeared. Only the lump on my hand is still there." As we had been expecting any day to hear of her death, my sister, who was listening to the conversation, told me to ask her what saint she had been praying to. She answered that she hadn't prayed to anyone. And my sister Felisa said, "Well, tell her that I have, that *I* prayed for her to Father Josemaría Escrivá."

It was in this simple way that Sister Concepción learned that she owed her new lease on life to the intercession of the founder of Opus Dei. From then on, she was very grateful to him. She recalled that a relative of hers had asked her to pray for Opus Dei back in the 1940s, and since then she had done so frequently. Sister Pilar, who was her close companion during the last years of her life, bears witness to Sister Concepción's complete conviction that she owed her cure to the intercession of the founder of Opus Dei: "Sister considered it a matter of justice to recognize his intercession. God had granted her sisters' petition through the intercession of Msgr. Josemaría Escrivá. She also regarded it as a sort of repayment for all the prayers she had said for Opus Dei over the last forty years of her life."

The doctors' judgment

As we have seen, some time passed before Sister Concepción's doctors learned of her sudden cure. She finally went to see the community's physician, Dr. José W., who after a clinical examination confirmed the disappearance of the tumors on her shoulder and foot. He ordered X-rays, which were taken on July 28, 1976, and then compared them with those from the previous year. As he pointed out in his testimony, what struck him was the total disappearance of the tumors; there remained only some areas of increased density representing deposits of calcium in the capsule of the shoulder joint.

To review this case briefly, the medical hypothesis during Sister Concepción's illness had been that she suffered from cancer with metastases. The bleeding gastric ulcer led them to suspect that this might in fact be the primary cancer. The lumps on her shoulder, foot, and hand would then be metastases. But the diagnosis was never completed because of the patient's precarious physical condition. The physicians did not want to risk even the minor operation of taking a sample for analysis. Furthermore, in view of the rapid progress of the illnesses, the doctors supposed that death was imminent. Accordingly, they decided to leave the patient in peace and gave her no treatment except for some analgesics to alleviate the severe pain.

With all of this in mind, the sudden and complete disappearance of the tumors might have meant that the real cause of Sister Concepción's condition had not been detected—unless a small residue could be found with which to carry out a histological analysis; this, indeed, is what happened. While the larger tumors (on the shoulder and foot) disappeared without leaving a trace, there remained a small nodule on her right thumb with which a biopsy could be performed. Since this growth could not properly be called a tumor, the physician who took the sample described it simply as "a local hardening where tumefaction had previously taken place." This nodule was providential, because the biopsy permitted an accurate diagnosis and demonstrated, as a consequence, that the patient's sudden restoration to health was medically inexplicable.

The specimen was taken in August 1976. Then, in October 1977 the remaining nodule, which still remained benign, was removed. Histological analysis revealed it to be lipomatosis, a condition that, even if benign, could cause serious complications depending on its size and location. Moreover, it could not be cured or be expected to regress spontaneously. The only practicable treatment of the nodule was surgical removal. The analysis also made it clear that the original tumors were unrelated to the patient's gastric illness.

The miraculous cure that night in June 1976 was not the end of the story. Simultaneous with the surprising disappearance of the tumors, Sister Concepción's general state of health began to improve rapidly. The gastric hemorrhages ceased just as suddenly, and all the other symptoms showed signs of improvement. Professor Eduardo Ortiz de Landázuri, a well-known Spanish internal medicine specialist who made a complete study of the case, told the archdiocesan tribunal: "From that night in June 1976, after the disappearance of the tumors on her left shoulder and the lumps on her left foot, the patient continued to make remarkable progress." By August 1976, only two months after her cure, Sister Concepción had already practically recovered from severe anemia, and the last X-ray examination (October 1977) revealed no trace of a gastric ulcer.

A niece of Sister Concepción who had visited her frequently during her illness observed her aunt's complete cure for herself a few months afterward. "I cannot be certain," she stated, "when her diet became less strict than when she had the ulcer. But I recall that she stayed with us over Christmas 1976 and even ate spiced sausage, which agreed with her. That same Christmas I had a baby, and Sister Concepción offered to take on the housework while looking after my four other children. She was well enough to help my mother with everything."

* * *

Sister Concepción Boullón lived twelve more years after her cure, which was declared miraculous by the Church. There was no recurrence of the two illnesses from which she had been cured through the intercession of the founder of Opus Dei. The statements made by all the witnesses (nuns, relatives, and doctors) were in complete agreement. During the remaining years of her life, Sister Concepción enjoyed a normal state of health for a person her age.

Toward the end, now more than eighty years of age, she showed symptoms of developing nephrosclerosis (a progressive aging of the renal tissue), as well as uremia (an increase of urea in the blood) and other symptoms common in old age. Attending physicians were unanimously of the opinion that these symptoms were unrelated to the afflictions from which she had been miraculously cured.

Sister Concepción Boullón died peacefully on November 22, 1988. The cause of death, according to the official medical certificate, was the chronic renal sclerosis from which she had been suffering. She was eighty-two when the Lord called her to himself. She did not have the joy of seeing the beatification of Msgr. Escrivá while still on earth, but we can suppose that she did rejoice with him in heaven.

2. Restoration of Vision

"Swift, total cure of neuritis of the optic nerve." (March–April 1979)[6]

This chapter reports the inexplicable cure of a serious form of neuritis of the optic nerve that had caused a sixteen-year-old boy to lose virtually all of his eyesight in a few short weeks.

To understand what happened in this case, it is necessary to recall that the retina is like a complex television antenna that collects light. The optic nerve transmits these stimuli to the brain, where they are interpreted and integrated by a complex nerve-structure in the occipital lobe. The result is normal vision of objects as they are in reality, from the perspective of the viewer.

Using a familiar comparison, the optic nerve is like the cable that connects a television antenna (or, in the case of cable television, the transmitter) to the television set. Just as a malfunction of the cable would affect the quality of images on the screen, similarly, malfunction of the optic nerve adversely affects the information reaching the brain and impairs vision.

One of the principal disorders of the optic nerve is neuritis, a severe condition that may have several possible causes producing similar symptoms: the patient suddenly experiences blurred vision in one or both eyes, often accompanied by pain or discomfort and a central scotoma, or black spot in the center of the field of vision. Usually one of the first signs of this progressive impairment of vision is the loss of color perception, sometimes resulting in simple black-and-white vision.

Acute and progressive loss of sight

Andrés, a sixteen-year-old student, was born in the United States in 1962 and moved with his Venezuelan parents to their home in that country at the age of two. There he grew up normally and attended primary and secondary schools. No

[6] This case is documented in *De fama signorum*, vol. 1, pp. 91–144, drawn up by the General Postulation of Opus Dei, dated May 1, 1991, and presented to the Congregation for the Causes of Saints.

family members had suffered eye diseases, with the exception of cataracts in his grandparents' old age.

In the fall of 1978, Andrés returned to the U.S. for the last year of high school and stayed with his older brother, Juan Carlos, a university student in Daytona Beach, Florida. The year began normally; Andrés got off to a good start and adapted well to his new environment, as his letters home attest. In February 1979, however, a progressive blurring of vision alarmed him, and Juan Carlos took him to an optometrist, who prescribed glasses. In the following weeks his eyesight continued to deteriorate rapidly. The glasses were of no use, and Andrés found it necessary to use a magnifying glass to read and write. In a few weeks he went almost entirely blind.

At first neither Andrés nor his brother paid much attention to something that they attributed to a heavier use of the eyes. But as his brother's eyesight rapidly worsened, Juan Carlos began to be concerned. When he discovered that Andrés could no longer distinguish between red and green traffic lights, Juan Carlos would not allow him to ride his new motorbike and wrote home about what was happening to his brother. What most alarmed their parents was a letter from Andrés at the end of March. When they compared it with one he had written two months earlier, there was an astonishing difference: the second letter was written in such large script that their son's handwriting was no longer recognizable. They decided that his father, Roberto, should go to Florida right away and investigate the advisability of finding a specialist.

An alarming diagnosis

Roberto made a written record of his son's condition between April 8 and 16, a crucial week in its development:

On April 8, 1979, Palm Sunday, Roberto flew to Florida and went directly to the Bascom Palmer hospital in Miami, one of the best known facilities in the South. Normally, appointments are made several months in advance, but Roberto insisted that Andrés be seen immediately because of the seriousness of his condition. On the 11th, Wednesday in Holy Week, Andrés underwent a long series of eye examinations at the hospital. His father, who had worn glasses ever since boyhood, observed: "Before that sad day I'd never seen so many ophthalmological instruments or so many specialists at one time. They examined my son minutely for eight hours without a break (and I say 'they' because I saw him attended by at least five specialists)."

The last examination that day was a test for color vision. The form they were handed simply read, "Probably Leber." Roberto was told, "Take your son home. For the moment we cannot prescribe anything. Bring him back next month for further tests. We think he has Leber."

Such an infirmity was unknown to Roberto, but he soon discovered that Leber's disease is a hereditary atrophy of the optic nerve, "a devastating and little-understood form of optic neuritis occurring predominantly in males after puberty," according to a standard ophthalmological textbook. It continues: "Eyesight deteriorates rapidly or quite suddenly in a relatively short space of time. Loss of vision is often asymmetric to begin with, first in one eye and then in the other. In almost all cases central vision is selectively affected." Leber's disease differs from other forms of optic neuritis in that "it is bilateral, hereditary, not recurrent, and does not go into remission. In cases of this disease the central scotomata do not disappear, and vision is permanently impaired."

Roberto's anguish, on learning that the disease from which his son was probably suffering had no known treatment and would inevitably lead to blindness, can readily be appreciated. On the evening of that same day, Roberto phoned a family friend in New York, a woman whose son was an ophthalmologist. With their help he obtained an appointment for April 17 at one of the best-known eye hospitals in New York, the New York Eye and Ear Institute.

A general mobilization of prayers

Roberto recalled some encouraging words in the phone conversation with his friend in New York: "Don't give up hope. Pray for him to Msgr. Escrivá. Just you wait, God will cure Andrés for you through his intercession." At that point, Roberto says, "All I knew about Msgr. Escrivá was that he had founded Opus Dei, and I had once skimmed through his book *The Way*. But I prayed to him for my son with all my heart."

He also phoned his wife in Caracas to relate this advice in the context of the medical opinion and to suggest that she pray to God through the intercession of Msgr. Escrivá. This news mobilized the whole family to pray earnestly for Andrés' cure. His mother also phoned a friend of hers in Opus Dei who consoled her and promised to pray and get others to pray for the same intention. The friend added that prayer for the intercession of the Servant of God should be offered with great faith.

Easter Sunday came and went, and on the evening of the following day, April 16, Roberto arrived in New York with Andrés. The boy could not even watch television because the colors and images were so blurred. After dinner with the friends who had arranged for the appointment, Roberto was given a card with the prayer for private devotion to the founder of Opus Dei. He writes, "When we got back to the hotel I said the prayer with all the faith I could muster."

A profound change

The next day, at 9 A.M., Andrés and his father arrived at the hospital to begin the same kind of tests that he had received in Miami. The friend who had arranged for them on such short notice, a member of the hospital staff, later told Roberto that in the course of the day the doctors also spoke several times with the specialists who had seen his son in Miami in order to exchange opinions and compare observations.

There were striking differences in their views of the situation. Roberto explains: "At 3 P.M. Dr. Thomas M., the head specialist, told me, 'Your son has nothing wrong with his eyes. If the Miami diagnosis was correct, there's been a miracle here. Take him with you, don't worry, and don't do anything to him, because two months from now he'll be perfectly fine.' "

"We didn't do anything further and took Andrés back to Venezuela for a long holiday. He lost that whole term because he had been unable to study for the exams. We went on praying to Msgr. Escrivá, and at the beginning of September he returned to school in the United States. He'd left his glasses in Miami and the magnifying glass at home. According to the letter he wrote to us on September 30, 1979, the marks he got at the end of the first month of school—like the ones he is earning now—show how good his vision has been."

Andrés was completely cured. That period of nearly total blindness was only a bad memory, like waking up after a nightmare. The urgent prayers that had gone up to heaven between April 8 and 16 invoking the intercession of the founder of Opus Dei had achieved what had seemed impossible.

The specialists' opinion

The head of the medical team at the New York hospital had said, "If the Miami diagnosis was correct, there's been a miracle here." As we saw, Leber's disease is incurable and progressive. There can be no doubt about the competence of the ophthalmological staff and the carefulness of the tests carried out in the Miami hospital. Everything was well documented by the five specialists over a period of eight hours.

The only thing about Andrés' clinical history that does not accord with other cases of Leber's disease is the absence of any family history of it. As described in textbooks, Leber's disease is hereditary, probably a recessive trait linked to the X-chromosome. In its absence, the Florida ophthalmologists noted a *probable* Leber, since Andrés' symptoms clearly indicated it and other possible causes of neuritis of the optic nerve—toxins, infectious illnesses, multiple sclerosis or local sclerosis, metabolism disorders, etc.—had been discounted due to the absence of other symptoms accompanying such disorders.

The Postulation summoned two experts in ophthalmology to study the case in depth. Both concluded that in the absence of a family history of the disease it would be difficult to be certain about the diagnosis of Leber's disease in Andrés; but there was no doubt of an acute infection of the optic nerve of an otherwise unknown cause. Both examiners emphasized that what was really inexplicable was the rapidity of recovery. Within a week (between the tests carried out at the two hospitals), there was a swing of 180 degrees. Dr. Vicente B., a Spanish ophthalmologist, stated simply that "no natural causes could account for such a rapid recovery from such an illness."

Dr. José P., the other expert, set forth the only two possible alternatives: (1) It really was a case of Leber's disease (atypical, because of the absence of family antecedents), and this would normally have developed into complete atrophy of the optic nerve; or (2) it was not Leber's disease, in which case the actual cause of the neuritis would have to be identified to make a proper prognosis. Thus the exact truth cannot be determined. Considering the patient's age, the specialist inclined toward a possible toxic origin and added, "In such cases, the patient might recover without any treatment, though this would be highly unusual over such a short space of time."

Whatever the cause, the persons chiefly involved have no doubt that the cure resulted from divine intervention. The account of Andrés' father concludes: "Skeptics will say that the illness was merely the result of emotional factors—a fashionable explanation for everything these days. Others, less reluctant to believe, will speak of 'a very special favor.' But for my family and many people close to us, and most of all for my wife and me, who lived through those terrible days, it was nothing less than a great miracle granted by God, our Father, through Msgr. Escrivá's intercession."

3. A Vocation Saved

"Instant cure of a cloistered nun's irreversible deafness." (July 3, 1985)[7]

Blessed Josemaría's biographers document his great affection for people in religious life. He revered them, prayed for them, and asked others to do the same. His own calling differed from theirs, but whenever those who came to him for spiritual guidance showed signs of having a vocation to the religious life, he was happy to help them find their way.

He felt special esteem for cloistered religious. On his pastoral journeys contemplative communities in the various countries often invited him to visit to strengthen them with his priestly encouragement. He never turned down these invitations, and in many parlors of convents and monasteries he spoke enthusiastically about fidelity to the vocational commitment, asked for prayers, and referred to religious as "the Church's treasure."

Blessed Josemaría made it a daily practice to ask God for an increase of vocations among contemplative souls in every state and situation of life, and specifically in consecrated life. Countless religious men and women reciprocated by praying for Opus Dei and its apostolate in the world. And as the following account demonstrates, they continue to entrust their spiritual and material needs to Blessed Josemaría, knowing him now as an effective intercessor in heaven.

A convent of Discalced Carmelites

Sister Dora T. was born in Ecuador in 1955, the fifth in a family of ten brothers and sisters. She was a Carmelite novice when the events to be related here occurred. She had entered the convent a short while before, convinced that God was calling her to a life of renunciation and sacrifice according to the spirit and rules of St. Teresa of Ávila.

One day in April 1985, having had a high temperature

[7] This case is documented in *De fama signorum*, vol. 1, pp. 347–402.

caused by influenza, she noticed a sudden and complete loss of hearing in her right ear. She immediately informed the Prioress and other nuns, who gave her first aid, expecting the deafness to be temporary, but the remedies were of no avail. After several days a nurse who was superior of a neighboring home for the elderly was called to syringe Sister Dora's ear canal in the event it was blocked by wax. This was done and drops added, but the deafness persisted.

Next the Prioress summoned Dr. Francisco P., an ear, nose, and throat specialist, who confirmed the deafness and prescribed medication, some to be applied externally and some to be taken orally. When several check-ups found Sister Dora's condition unchanged, another specialist, Dr. Oscar V., was consulted. After a thorough examination, he advised that the patient see a specialist in Quito, where better means were available to make an accurate diagnosis.

"Pray to Msgr. Escrivá"

After three and a half months, Sister Dora became concerned not only for her health, but because her deafness might be an impediment to her religious profession. The Prioress confirmed this in her written testimony: "Sister Dora Matilde was dismayed at the prospect of continuing deafness and deeply distressed by the possibility that this might prevent her from following her vocation. . . ."

The Prioress shared this distress, because her novice was showing signs of a true Carmelite vocation. This led her to begin entrusting Sister Dora's condition to the intercession of the Servant of God, Msgr. Escrivá. "I had read of many favors granted through his intercession in a magazine published by Opus Dei on Msgr. Escrivá, his holiness, and his work," she explained, adding that earlier her prayers for his intercession on behalf of a nephew had been heard. "This made me trust in the value of his intercession, and with the assurance of a humble and trusting faith, I advised Sister Dora Matilde to pray insistently to Msgr. Escrivá for the grace of a cure."

The Prioress and novice both decided to make a novena to him. According to Sister Dora, "To start the novena, Mother

Prioress lent me a little prayer card, and I copied out the prayer by hand. I returned the card to Mother Prioress, who looks after it as if it were a relic." Sister Dora continues: "I prayed that prayer two or three times a day, asking to be cured; at the same time, I told him that if he obtained this miracle it would be a sign that he wanted me to be a nun for the whole of my life. I also asked him to let me remain in the convent, because if I were outside I would be very unhappy. I also asked for an improvement in my health so that I could serve my Mothers better."

The Prioress realized that, along with fervent and trusting prayer, all available human means should also be used. Following the advice of Dr. V., she authorized Sister Dora to see Dr. Mauricio L., a renowned specialist who would perform the necessary examinations in the capital.

The first journey to Quito

Sister Dora traveled to Quito with her mother and one of her brothers. On June 27, 1985, an ear specialist made a detailed examination, which showed a total hearing loss in the right ear. Sister Dora could not even hear a piercing whistle in that ear. In light of this result and the clinical history, the diagnosis indicated a "sudden sensorineural deafness, probably caused by a virus." The specialist himself indicated in his written testimony why there was no point in attempting treatment: "Our experience in approximately fifty cases of sudden deafness, when studied in detail, showed that positive results were obtained only in patients who were treated within the first week of the onset of deafness, and that medical treatment proved ineffective where treatment began after more than a week. In view of this experience, we did not prescribe any medication."

To rule out any possibility that the deafness was due to a tumor, the specialist arranged for X-rays to be taken of the cranium, after which he would carry out other tests in an attempt to establish more precisely the cause of the deafness.

After reviewing the relevant literature, a specialist consulted by the Postulation concluded that "sudden sensorineural deafness occurring after upper respiratory viral diseases such as influenza is common, relative to the rarity of such cases." Recent research has shown that one of the ways such viruses reach the inner ear is through the middle ear when it becomes inflamed. In addition, the oval membrane (which separates the middle ear from the inner ear) can sometimes be ruptured by violent sneezing. It is also a proven fact that the membrane is permeable to toxins produced by viruses, which can infect the inner ear and cause injuries to the labyrinth. "These ruptures or tears in the round window membrane," explained the specialist who was consulted, "can heal spontaneously . . . although some loss of hearing always results. . . . The longer the time lapse since the deafness began, the worse the prognosis."

It had already been nearly three months since Sister Dora lost all hearing in her right ear. The prospects for even a partial recovery were not hopeful. The Quito specialist informed Sister Dora of this bad prognosis, and that same afternoon he repeated it to the Prioress when she phoned him. In her words: "He told me that regrettably there was nothing more to be done, since the deafness in the right ear had been confirmed, and there was no cure. Still, he thought it a good idea to have an X-ray taken in order to determine whether there might be a tumor. My trust in the Servant of God became deeper, now that her condition was humanly incurable. When I spoke to Sister, I encouraged her once more to strengthen her faith and continue the novena."

A sudden cure

Lacking the means to pay for the X-rays on that trip, Sister Dora postponed them and returned to the convent. Encouraged by her Prioress, she continued to ask Msgr. Escrivá's intercession for a miracle.

Six days later, on July 3, she returned to Quito with her brother. The X-rays could not be taken that morning, so she went back to the hospital again in the afternoon. Here is her account of what happened then: "While I was waiting for the consultation, I was suddenly able to hear everything clearly in my right ear, and in great surprise—in fact, indescribable amazement—I informed my brother." As the X-rays were no longer necessary, she immediately went to see the specialist who had previously examined her. His medical assistant first repeated the audiometric examination and, to his astonishment, confirmed that her deafness had disappeared. He immediately informed the specialist, who could not believe it and decided to carry out a fresh examination himself. The result was the same: normal hearing in the right ear.

In astonishment, the specialist, his assistant, and the attending nurse were only able to ask Sister Dora what saint she had invoked. She simply replied that it had been Msgr. Josemaría Escrivá. "I could not explain how such a poor person could receive such an extraordinary miracle," she wrote later. "With my heart full of gratitude, and moved to tears, I began in silence to recite as a hymn of thanksgiving, 'My soul magnifies the Lord. . . .' "

Shortly afterward, the Prioress phoned the doctor. "I asked anxiously about the consultation," her account continues. "The doctor told me what had happened. He hadn't yet recovered from his initial astonishment. He kept repeating that he didn't understand, but that it was nevertheless clearly a fact that the Sister could hear perfectly, that she had told him she had prayed to the founder of Opus Dei, and that a miracle had resulted."

The Prioress went on: "I cannot explain how moved I was spiritually. It was overwhelming that something supernatural had taken place in a humble novice of our community who had prayed for it with faith and trust. My whole being was an act of thanksgiving, with tears of emotion, inner self-annihilation, and prayers of praise and gratitude to God, who was glorifying his faithful servant, Msgr. Escrivá."

No human explanation

The Quito specialist who had diagnosed Sister Dora's deafness as irreversible and had objectively verified the fact of the sudden cure, concluded his testimony in these words: "In our experience, cases of sudden deafness that are not treated within seven days of onset do not improve, with or without treatment. We have no cases in our archives of patients in whom a profound sensorineural deafness has been found at one consultation, and a normal reading of the audiometer at the next consultation. Nevertheless, tonal audiometry is of a subjective nature; that is, it depends on the patient's response. In doubtful cases or where we suspect that the patient is giving false responses, we have recourse to objective methods independent of patient responses. In the present case such methods were unnecessary. We must therefore conclude that this cure has no scientific medical explanation."

Subsequently, Sister Dora's sudden cure was studied in the ENT department of a hospital in Quito. The final statement, signed by the department head toward the end of 1986, declares: "We conclude that this case has no real scientific explanation."

Prof. Carlos G., an ENT specialist, reached the same conclusion after examining the entire clinical documentation at the Postulation's request; he writes:

> I have studied the case.... The audiometric test only shows vestiges of hearing in the right ear, and the osseous canal of that ear is very damaged. The diagnosis is a profound sensorineural lack of hearing in that ear. In view of this patient's recovery of normal hearing after a few weeks, we are totally in agreement with Dr. Mauricio L. that there is no scientific explanation for this cure. In my experience, patients with sudden deafness of the sensorineural type have irreversible symptoms, even if they receive medical treatment, which was not even prescribed in this case.

Prof. Carlos M., head of another ENT department, agreed with his colleagues. After regretting that no objective tests had been carried out, which would have been able to measure how severely the inner ear had been affected, he concluded: "There is one thing that surprises me, and that is the abrupt and spontaneous recovery from deafness; generally recuperation is slower and gradual, depending on the extent of neurosensorial damage. Also unusual is the length of time between the onset of deafness and recovery from it."

Sister Dora does not hesitate to attribute her cure to the intercession of the founder of Opus Dei, to whom she had appealed with faith and an ardent desire to continue in her vocation to the full. She ends her testimony in these words: "I am very happy that Msgr. Josemaría Escrivá de Balaguer listened to my prayers, together with those of my Carmelite Mother and Sisters and those of my relatives, for now I can remain in the convent through the help of God's grace and Msgr. Josemaría's intercession. . . . It permits me to continue following my vocation, and every day I raise my soul in prayer to Msgr. Josemaría Escrivá de Balaguer, that he may listen to all who have recourse to him and look upon them with compassion."

Words of the Novice Mistress at the time of Sister Dora's cure provide a fitting conclusion to this report: "As Novice Mistress, I felt an inexpressible spiritual joy over this novice whose deafness required medical attention and today is able to hear perfectly well. She continues to entrust herself every day to the founder of Opus Dei with very great faith, regarding him as her 'doctor,' both spiritually and materially. He was responsible for this miracle when, humanly speaking, nothing more could be done. Those of us who witnessed it call her 'the miracle Sister,' but it was all due to grace!"

4. A Widow's Plea

"Sudden recovery from a severe stricture of the esophagus." (April 21, 1986)[8]

This story comes from Australia. It centers on Klara V., who was born in the former Yugoslavia in 1936. She moved to Sydney in 1965 and was widowed in 1974. At the time of these events, three younger children still lived with her at home, while the eldest daughter had married.

What stands out in her case is God's immediate response to a widowed mother's plea for help. Blessed Josemaría's rapid intervention as soon as Klara invoked his intercession is reminiscent of our Lord's tender compassion for the widow of Naim (Lk 7: 11–17) and his affectionate attention to the poor widow at the Temple treasury in Jerusalem (Lk 21: 1–4). These Gospel episodes had so impressed the founder of Opus Dei that he commented on them again and again, drawing attention to God's merciful love for his people. On numerous occasions the founder himself imitated that example by addressing words of consolation to widows, encouraging them always to trust in God, who will "not ignore the supplication of the fatherless, nor the widow when she pours out her story" (Sir 35: 14).

An accident at home

Klara's grave distress resulted from an accident at home in 1955, when she still lived in Yugoslavia. She recalls it in her testimony addressed to the Postulation: "When I was nineteen years old and living in Subotica, Yugoslavia, I felt thirsty one evening about 9 o'clock, and took two sips from what appeared to be a carbonated drink on a shelf in the kitchen. I immediately realized, in terror, that it was a concentrated liquid used for washing floors."

This was a type of caustic soda sold in solid form and dissolved in water to make the concentrate, which could then be

[8] The details of this case are documented in *De fama signorum*, vol. 1, pp. 657–680.

diluted in proportions of one cup per pail of water. Even in that diluted form, the soda was still strong enough to cause Klara's hands to bleed if some of it got on them whenever she used it for cleaning. "What I drank was the concentrate."

She was rushed to the hospital vomiting blood because of the extreme abrasion of the esophagus. Her condition was so serious that the doctors feared she would not survive the night. Thank God, this was not the case. When she recovered, an esophagoscopy showed irreversible damage due to chemical burns. Once scars had formed, the diameter of the esophagus had declined from the normal measurement of 1.6 inches to about 1.3. Attempts to dilate it were unsuccessful.

At first Klara could not take any food; gradually she managed to swallow some liquids and very soft foods. After a month she began to suffer spasms of the esophagus at mealtime, and these became real torture. Buscopan (a well-known antispasm drug) was prescribed twenty minutes prior to each meal. She was informed that no other treatment was available. The situation was medically irreversible.

After two months she was able to return home to begin a Calvary that lasted more than thirty years. In spite of the medication, "nearly every day the food got stuck in my esophagus," she writes, "so that I either had to disgorge it or wait until it slowly went down. At regular intervals, once a week on average, I suffered spasms, which generally lasted several hours. During that interval I could not eat anything or even swallow. Twice in the last ten years the spasms were especially prolonged, lasting from thirty-six to forty hours."

Over time Klara abstained from certain foods that caused particular distress, and even with the Buscopan her meals were prolonged ordeals. This, together with the ever-present risk of vomiting, meant she could never eat in restaurants or with anyone outside the family.

Thirty years later

One day in April 1986, Klara's youngest son brought home a booklet about the Servant of God, Msgr. Josemaría Escrivá, which he had found in church there in Sydney. At first his mother did not pay much attention to this publication of the Opus Dei Vice-Postulation Office in Australia, because of her poor reading ability in English. When her son explained it to her, she asked him to pray to the Servant of God for her. One of her other children told her about the favors attributed to Msgr. Escrivá's intercession that were reported in the booklet. This awakened Klara's faith.

Here is her account of what followed at a precise moment closely connected to her invocation of the founder of Opus Dei:

> On the morning of Monday, April 21, 1986, I picked up the booklet, looked at the prayer for private devotion . . . and read it. I could not understand all the words, but as I read I felt that God was going to help me. That very afternoon, I tried to eat some sweets I had made for the children. I found that I could swallow them easily, something I usually found very hard. And just at that moment I realized I had forgotten to take the Buscopan. I was amazed.
>
> That evening, I was about to eat some chicken I had prepared with a Hungarian recipe. I told my children what had happened in the afternoon and asked whether they thought I should take the Buscopan or not. One of them said, "Mum, if you have faith, don't take it." I didn't take it, and I was able to eat without any problem.

In 1988, in her second report to the Postulation, Klara wrote:

> Since that day I have not taken Buscopan, and I have experienced practically no difficulty in eating. Only on five or six occasions, when I did not take the precaution of eating slowly and chewing properly, did the food stick in my esophagus, sometimes resulting in spasms lasting from five to twenty minutes. On those occasions, if the spasms didn't stop, I put the prayer card of Msgr. Escrivá on my breast and said the prayer, with the Our Father, Hail Mary, and Glory Be, and the spasms would stop after a few minutes. Now I can eat everything, even foods that for many years I had been unable to swallow."

Klara's children, who had seen their mother suffer for so many years, attribute without hesitation this prodigious and permanent cure to the intercession of the founder of Opus Dei. The report of her son John, signed also by his two brothers, reads: "Now she eats everything, including those foods she could not have before, and she has not had any more spasms. It seems to be something extraordinary, not only because of the cure of an ailment she suffered for many years, but also because in April 1986 she stopped the medicine she had been taking all that time."

Of special interest is the testimony of Dr. Elizabeth H., for thirteen years Klara's family doctor, who was, of course, familiar with the case history. Dr. H. ruled out any possibility that medication produced the cure: "I prescribed Buscopan to reduce the likelihood of spasms, but there was never any hope that this medicine could be a cure." In her report, dated in 1989, Dr. H. states that without doubt the sudden disappearance of this affliction is medically inexplicable. "Shortly after April 1986," she wrote,

> Klara told me that beginning on a precise day that month she had no difficulty in swallowing and that the spasms had disappeared, in spite of having stopped taking the Buscopan. I found this surprising, because I have never known anyone in Klara's situation who experienced such an immediate and lasting improvement. Only once in the past three years—May 10, 1989—did she have a long bout of spasms, which required an injection of Buscopan and Valium. In spite of that, I consider the three years of remission without the use of Buscopan extraordinary.

Klara attributes the disappearance of her symptoms to Blessed Josemaría's intercession: "I am sure," she says, "that this impressive and unexpected improvement is due to Msgr. Escrivá's intercession. Since the day of my cure, I have invoked him before every meal, asking him to help me eat without difficulty, and thanking him at the end."

5. An assault and a cancer

"Two cases of exceptionally swift and lasting cures
in the same person." (1986 and 1987)[9]

On December 27, 1985, a terrorist group struck Schwechat Airport in Vienna. Hand grenades and a hail of machine-gun bullets caused panic among passengers waiting to board their flights. Wolfgang K., a fifty-year-old physics teacher, was in the airport at the time. Seriously wounded by bullets and shrapnel, he underwent emergency surgery at a nearby hospital in a seven-hour operation. The next day complications brought him to death's door. But in spite of a dire prognosis, he made an astonishing recovery, and less than three weeks later (January 15, 1986) he was able to drive home in his own car.

A year later, Wolfgang had a routine medical check-up. Although he felt perfectly well, prostate cancer was discovered, with widespread metastasis in the lungs and pelvis. Treatment began immediately, and again with remarkable results; in only four months the cancer was in complete remission.

Wolfgang and his family attribute these two favors to the intercession of Msgr. Escrivá, to whom they prayed with great faith. The miraculous nature of both cures is not so much the outcome, for correct treatment had been applied immediately, but the extraordinary speed with which they occurred.

An extremely serious condition

When Wolfgang was admitted to the hospital after the terrorist attack, the diagnosis included perforation of the left lung with haemothorax (heavy loss of blood in the pleural cavity); contusion of the right lung; an abdominal wound with iliac perforation and no exit wound; additional bullet wounds with incrustation on the right tibia and mandible.

The operation was expertly performed on the major injuries—thorax, abdomen and tibia. Nevertheless, serious com-

[9] The facts of this case are documented in *De fama signorum*, vol. 2, pp. 7–56.

plications developed within the first twenty-four hours, not unexpectedly, in view of the magnitude of the trauma. Pulmonary insufficiency required artificial respiration; isostenuria and heavy polyuria indicated renal failure; and there was a build-up of bile due to hepatic insufficiency with colestasis.

Medical statistics for multiple injuries producing acute failure in any system or organ indicate a mortality rate of 20 percent, rising to 30 to 40 percent if it is a lung, and to 50 to 80 percent for any additional organs. In the present case, then, life expectancy was between 20 and 50 percent. In comparable cases, intensive care would normally follow for three or four weeks, so long as there were no further complications (infection, pulmonary laceration, pulmonary embolism). Thereafter a patient would remain under ordinary hospital care, followed by four weeks of rehabilitation.

To summarize, if all went well, such complex traumas would require four or five weeks of hospitalization, with the first three or four in intensive care, and then about the same amount of time for rehabilitation. In the present case, however, the patient stayed in intensive care for just twelve days and then one more week in the hospital. A recovery that would normally take a month or more took only half that time, even with complications.

Wolfgang's relatives and friends believe this happy outcome of a life-threatening assault was due to the intercession of Josemaría Escrivá, to whom many had turned from the day it occurred.

A surprising improvement after nine days

As soon as she received the news of the attack and the gravity of her uncle's wounds, his niece spontaneously invoked the founder of Opus Dei because of her knowledge of his reputation for holiness. Very soon many other relatives and friends joined in her prayer. During the first week, when the patient was in critical condition, these prayers continued incessantly. Friedrich K., Wolfgang's brother, offered the following testimony as Professor of Internal Medicine at the University of Vienna and Chief of the Internal Medicine department at one of the city's hospitals: "His wife and many relatives prayed without interruption. A great number of the faithful of Opus Dei who knew my brother, lay people and priests, made a novena to the Servant of God. . . . On the ninth day a surprising improvement took place, so that twelve days after the event the patient could be moved from intensive care to the hospital's general ward of internal medicine."

On January 4, nine days after the attack, the artificial respirator was removed. Since the X-rays still showed atelectasia (a collapsed zone) in the upper lobe of the left lung and the patient also had hypoxemia (an oxygen deficiency in the blood), attending physicians continued intermittent oxygen respiration for three more days. In spite of the serious state of the lungs, especially the left one, none of the usual complications in such cases ensued.

An even more astonishing improvement occurred in the following days. On January 10, only two weeks after his admission, Wolfgang was able to get out of bed, and five days later he drove home from the hospital to continue rehabilitation there. He used a cane to ease the pressure on an ankle injury, but a week later he went to a dance, and a month after that he took fourth place in an alpine skiing competition with twenty participants.

Wolfgang's brother speaks for all who attributed his rapid recovery to the intercession of Opus Dei's founder: "In view of the danger to his life, this sudden and permanent cure must be attributed to divine intervention through the intercession of Josemaría Escrivá."

A year later

A year after his recovery, Wolfgang underwent a routine physical examination to assure himself that the damaged organs were functioning normally. He felt well and was back at work, teaching and doing research, along with regular exercise in tennis, gymnastics, and skiing. The examination, however, detected another life-threatening development completely unrelated to the incident of the year before.

When X-rays revealed numerous spots on the lungs—

probable indications of metastasis of a cancer of unknown origin—the doctors tried to trace the primary tumor by performing various analyses. Radiological examination with radioactive isotopes showed other metastases in all the pelvic bones. Then a PSA test (prostate specific antigen) found the cause: prostate activity was eighty times greater than normal. Further tests confirmed the diagnosis: "Highly malignant prostatic carcinoma, with widespread pulmonary and bone metastases."

Hormonal treatment and chemotherapy began at once and continued for four months. During this time Wolfgang continued working normally. At the end of the four months, X-rays showed that the pulmonary spots and the signs of bone metastases had disappeared completely; the blood count was normal. The test for prostatic activity was also normal. In view of these results, chemotherapy was suspended, but hormonal treatment continued.

Wolfgang's doctors declared the result to be extraordinarily exceptional, considering that the metastases had affected organs previously damaged in the terrorist attack. Clinical experience shows that a cancer with these characteristics (after an initial positive reaction to treatment in 40 percent of the cases) normally recurs and leads to death after two or three years in 80 percent of the cases. In Wolfgang's case, analyses carried out four years later showed that the cure was complete and permanent. "This outcome is so unusual," Professor K. declared, "that it was decided to go back and verify the accuracy of the first diagnosis. It proved to be wholly accurate, and also the judgment about what stage the illness had reached."

This time, too, Wolfgang's relatives and friends were convinced of the supernatural intervention of the founder of Opus Dei, to whom many had made one novena after another as soon as they learned of the cancer and its prognosis.

6. No More Children

"The pregnancy of an infertile woman." (April, 1988)[10]

The Old Testament relates several miraculous conceptions and childbirths granted by God in response to the trusting and persevering prayers of infertile women. For the Israelites and other ancient peoples, offspring was a clear sign of God's blessing, and sterility was therefore considered a disgrace.

The story of Elkanah's wife Hannah, as told in the First Book of Samuel, is a good example. Hannah was barren, and every year when she went up to the Temple with her husband, Elkanah's other wife would reproach her because of her infertility. "Therefore Hannah wept and would not eat. And Elkanah, her husband, said to her, 'Hannah, why do you weep? And why do you not eat? And why is your heart sad? Am I not more to you than ten sons?' " (1 Sam 1: 7–8). Hannah did not answer. "The Lord had closed her womb," as Scripture puts it, and nothing on earth could console her.

But Hannah was also a devout woman. On one of their annual journeys to the Temple, after offering the ritual sacrifice, "she prayed to the Lord, and wept bitterly. And she made a vow and said, 'O Lord of hosts, if thou wilt indeed look on the affliction of thy maidservant, and remember me, and not forget thy maidservant, but wilt give to thy maidservant a son, then I will give him to the Lord all the days of his life' " (1 Sam 1: 11). God heard her prayer, and a year later she conceived a son. When the child had grown, she took him to the Temple that he might serve God "all the days of his life." This child was Samuel, one of the great prophets of Israel. Afterward, Hannah bore three more sons and two daughters, because "nothing is impossible with God" (Lk 1: 37), the Lord of life and death.

In our times God continues to work wonders that echo Biblical times, for example, a sterile woman who conceives and gives birth by natural means. Blessed Josemaría wrote, "God is

[10] The details of this case are documented in *De fama signorum*, vol. 2, pp. 59-88.

ever the same. What is lacking are men of faith. Supply that need and there will be a renewal of the wonders we read of in the Gospel. *Ecce non est abbreviata manus Domini*: God's arm, his power, has not grown weaker!" (*The Way*, no. 586).

The following story is one such instance of God's power and greatness, for he listens to the boldest supplications when they are addressed to him with faith and love and in complete submission to his most loveable will.

An illness that caused sterility

Pilar C. was born in Chile in 1954. Having grown up in a Catholic family of nine children, she wanted to have a large family herself. In 1976 she married Alfredo C., who also came from a Catholic family. A year after the wedding they were delighted when their love bore fruit and Pilar gave birth to a son who was given the same name as his father at Baptism. "We were hoping he would be the first of many," writes Alfredo, but "a year later my wife contracted an illness that made it impossible for her to have more children. This was very hard for us to accept, so with our hope still intact we consulted the best specialists in the country. The diagnosis was always unfavorable. Nevertheless, Pilar underwent several operations, always hoping the problem could be corrected, but it was all in vain. Her illness was incurable."

The doctors had diagnosed endometritis, a condition that leads to progressive sterility due to the hormonal alterations it causes, as well as resulting inflammations in the uterus, ovaries, and fallopian tubes. In spite of the treatments, Pilar's illness steadily advanced. In April 1986, surgery was required; a left salpingectomy (surgical removal of the left fallopian tube and ovary) was performed and a cyst removed from the right ovary. The intestine had to be detached in numerous places where it was adhering to the right ovary. The right fallopian tube also showed a pathological dilation, which reduced its possibility of capturing the ovum at the time of ovulation, as pregnancy requires.

This operation made it virtually impossible for Pilar and Alfredo to have children in the natural way, as her doctor explained. He went on to suggest that they might attempt in vitro fertilization, where the embryo is subsequently transferred to the mother's womb. As practicing Catholics, Pilar and Alfredo knew that the Church objects to such procedures on moral grounds. They decided instead to place all their trust in God, whose will they accepted.

Following the advice of Blessed Josemaría

Pilar and Alfredo were guided at every moment by the advice Blessed Josemaría had given in similar cases. During an interview in 1968,[11] a journalist asked the founder of Opus Dei the following question: "In your opinion, what meaning should Christian couples who are childless give to their married life?" Here is his response, worth quoting in full:

> In the first place I would tell them that they should not give up hope too easily. They should ask God to give them children and, if it is His will, to bless them as He blessed the patriarchs of the Old Testament. And then it would be good for both of them to see a good doctor. If in spite of everything God does not give them children, they should not regard themselves as being thwarted. They should be happy, discovering in this very fact God's will for them. Often God does not give children because He is asking for more. God asks them to put the same effort and the same kind and gentle dedication into helping their neighbors, as they would have put into raising their children, without the human joy that comes from having children of one's own. There is, then, no reason to feel they are failures or to give in to sadness.
>
> If the married couple have interior life, they will understand that God is urging them to make of their lives a generous Christian service, a different apostolate from the one they would have fulfilled with their children, but an equally marvelous one. If they look around they will discover people who need help, charity and love. There are,

[11] *Conversations with Monsignor Escrivá de Balaguer* (Shannon: Ecclesia Press, 1968), p. 115.

> moreover, many apostolic tasks at which they can work. If they give themselves generously to others and forget themselves, if they put their hearts into their work, they will be wonderfully fruitful and will experience a spiritual parenthood that will fill their souls with true peace" (*Conversations*, no. 96).

Despite the medical opinion, Pilar maintained hope for several years that one day she could give birth to more children. Her hope was sustained by an appeal for the intercession of Josemaría Escrivá, "because of the affection I have for his Work, Opus Dei, and for him as a priest, and because I had the good fortune of having been at get-togethers with him when he came to Chile. Also because I know him through his books and writings, and because . . . I consider myself his spiritual daughter."

Many others joined her in asking him for the same intention, as Bernardita J., one of her friends, recalls: "Her sisters, parents, husband, friends, and even some cloistered nuns whom I asked to pray for an intention, all invoked Msgr. Escrivá to intercede for something that was humanly impossible."

As the years passed the couple continued to wait patiently. Eventually Pilar remembered what Opus Dei's founder had said: "God may have other plans." She explains in her testimony that after eight years of persevering prayer for her special intention, "I resigned myself to the fact that I could not have more children, and so I no longer prayed for this intention, with the thought that God must want something different from me—for example, to dedicate myself to other people, which I could easily do, since I had only one child of my own."

It turned out, however, that God had been waiting too—for Pilar to make this act of total acceptance of his will—before granting the gift she had so longed for.

An inexplicable birth

Everything happened in the most natural way. In 1988 Pilar found herself pregnant. Her own surprise and that of her husband was exceeded, if possible, by the astonishment of her gynecologist, who knew very well how extremely unlikely it was for this to happen. The pregnancy progressed normally, and on January 9, 1989, Juan José was born by Cesarean section. One of those who witnessed his birth affirms that the attending physician "declared emphatically that there was no human explanation for it, as Pilar continued to be as infertile as when he had begun to treat her."

The medical record expresses the surgeon's astonishment in these simple words: "There is no logical explanation for this pregnancy." The reasons supporting his statement are set forth in a subsequent account (June 1989), where the specialist describes the patient's one remaining ovary and one remaining fallopian tube, which he observed directly while performing the procedure: "The one remaining ovary . . . is almost totally covered by scar tissue, leaving only a small segment of it visible. Moreover, the fallopian tube cannot be clearly identified; there is an aperture which may correspond to the rim [of the tube], fixed in a position some distance from the ovary, which means that it is technically impossible for the ovum to fuse with the spermatozoon and begin the process of life which originated this pregnancy."

Anyone with a good knowledge of anatomy and physiology can see that a pregnancy in such circumstances is absolutely inexplicable. This conclusion was reached by Professor Luis C., head of Gynecology and Obstetrics at a well-known hospital in Madrid, whom the Postulation requested to investigate the case: "With the available data, and based on my personal experience and the written material I have thoroughly reviewed, one can only conclude that there is no scientific explanation for the fact that fertilization took place under those conditions."

One more fact needs to be added: Juan José was born on Blessed Josemaría's birthday. While the attending physician had no idea of that date's special significance when he arranged for the Cesarean section, Pilar and Alfredo saw in it a sign that they owed their child to the intercession before God of Opus Dei's founder. As one of the witnesses put it, it was like the "finishing touch" to a wonderful event that revealed the great goodness of the Author of life.

Pilar herself declares: "The miracle is that I had a child after being told by the doctors that there was no possibility of conceiving, except through 'in vitro fertilization,' which I rejected because I did not wish to disobey the Church. Nor was I receiving any special treatment; in fact, two years earlier I had undergone surgery that resulted in the following diagnosis: Fertilization is impossible through normal natural processes."

Without hesitation she attributes the conception and birth of her child to the intercession of Opus Dei's founder, to whom she had prayed for so long.

7. An Amputation Spared

"The sudden cure of advanced gangrene." (February 12, 1992) [12]

The city of Caracas, capital of Venezuela, is rich in contrasts. Alongside residential areas one can find *ranchitos*, groups of very poor dwellings inhabited mainly by families who moved to the city from the countryside in search of a better life. The contrast is striking, at least to anyone unacquainted with Latin America's amazing diversity of peoples.

Although there is growing concern about extreme socioeconomic inequality, the basic needs of large sectors of the population continue to be unmet. Many of the faithful, including members of the Opus Dei Prelature, are taking an active role in helping the underprivileged. Whether individually or in association with apostolic enterprises on behalf of the needy, they are fulfilling Blessed Josemaría's tireless efforts to teach and show by his example that "there is only one race, the race of the children of God."

A bicycle accident

Bombilla de Petare is one of those *ranchitos*. It is home to Rosa C., a young black woman, married and the mother of four: Tito, Juan, Grecia, and Roomel. She works in the clinic of Dr. Luis M., a surgeon who contributes his professional services to the people of Petare.

This story is about a four-year-old girl named Grecia. At 11 A.M. on Saturday, February 8, 1992, one of Grecia's brothers was giving her a ride in the carrier of a bicycle. Suddenly the front wheel hit a half-open manhole, causing the heavy manhole cover to strike the little girl's left foot, which began to bleed profusely. Her brother carried her straight home, where their mother held the foot under a running tap. As the wound

[12] The facts of this and the following cases are documented with photocopies of all the clinical tests, X-rays, and hospital reports. They are contained in *De fama signorum post beatificationem*, vol. 2, pp. 7–92, prepared by the General Postulation of Opus Dei on June 26, 1997, and presented to the Congregation for the Causes of Saints.

continued to bleed, she wrapped her daughter's foot in a towel, and a neighbor helped carry her to a medical clinic nearby.

On Saturdays those clinics serve a larger number of people and, not surprisingly, Rosa had to wait her turn. Eventually, a staff member routinely cleaned the child's wound and sutured it, giving it no special importance. At the insistence of Rosa and her husband, an X-ray was taken; it showed fractures of the second and third toe. Anti-inflammatories and antipyretics were prescribed, and Grecia was taken back home.

The following day, February 9, the front part of Grecia's foot was badly inflamed, and when Rosa saw a yellowish discharge, she took her back to the clinic. The staff prescribed antibiotics, but by evening the child had a temperature of 102 degrees Fahrenheit.

When there was no improvement on the following day, Rosa took Grecia to Dr. Luis M.'s surgical clinic. At 1:30 in the afternoon he examined the little patient and found her whole foot swollen, discolored, and in generally bad condition; her temperature had risen to 103 degrees. "The foot was very swollen," the doctor writes, "and blackish in color, looking dreadful. . . . The mother also brought me the X-ray. . . . It looked like a case of gangrene. I said to her mother: 'Rosa, this looks very bad to me; I hope we don't have to amputate her toe,' although inwardly I was hoping it would not be the whole foot."

The doctor proceeded to administer intramuscular injections of antibiotics and anti-inflammatories and took Grecia to the J. J. de los Rios Children's Hospital in Caracas, where the foot was drained and a sample taken of the fluid. The examining physician decided to admit her immediately for treatment of the fracture and blistering cellulitis on the back of the foot. Antibiotics were administered intravenously. Naturally, Rosa remained at her daughter's bedside.

The next day, the physicians informed Rosa that the only remedy was to amputate the two infected toes, because the gangrene was resistant to antibiotics. The longer the delay, the greater the danger that it would spread. Rosa continues the story: "That Tuesday morning, Dr. O., who was resident in the ward, called me aside. He asked me whether I was alone and I said I was; he told me they had to operate on the child to remove two toes because she had gangrene, and I should call my husband. . . . Dr. María Carmen, the one who spoke with me most, and another doctor said the same thing."

Grecia's parents, extremely distressed, could not decide whether to consent to the operation. It was only when Dr. Luis M. arrived that they signed the authorization form, for they had full trust in him. By then it was too late to perform the surgery that day, so it was scheduled for the following day.

The gangrene disappears

For a long time Rosa had been devoted to Msgr. Josemaría Escrivá and had encouraged others to have recourse to his intercession in times of difficulty. That day, seeing her distress, a friend encouraged her to place the child under the protection of the founder of Opus Dei: "The day before she had given me a prayer card of Msgr. Escrivá." Rosa adds:

> That Tuesday, in the evening, Tere said to me: "Rosa, pray to Msgr. Escrivá, and you will see how he helps you." But I took the prayer card and turned it head down, as though I was punishing him, and told him I was doing this because [it was said that] he only helped white people with plenty of money. Then I told him that he must take action to help me with my daughter because I worked for Dr. M., who has great devotion to him, and because I had gone for several years to his anniversary Masses in the church of the Chiquinquirá.

Then Rosa laid the prayer card on the child's foot and left it there all night, reciting the prayer over and over.

During that time, the unfounded assertion that Msgr. Escrivá helped only "white people with plenty of money" was being propagated by newspapers as the result of a campaign waged by a small number of people who had organized for the purpose of preventing his beatification, which was scheduled for May of that year. Rosa could see that the cure of her little daughter would refute that falsehood.

Early the next morning—Wednesday, February 12—Grecia was taken to the operating room. As the surgeon removed the bandage, he was surprised to find that the extensive inflammation of a few hours earlier had disappeared completely, along with the purplish color and the discharge. The gangrene was gone, and the operation was cancelled. Rosa continues:

> About an hour later they brought the child back, and the lady doctor asked me, "Who did your daughter's dressing yesterday?" I replied that nobody had touched the dressing. Then she told me they were not going to operate on my daughter because there was no need for it. . . . When they had unwrapped the dressing they asked me again, "Are you certain you didn't put anything on it?" And I repeated that no one had taken the dressing off.
>
> What surprised me most was that the doctor should say that somebody had changed her dressing in the night, when I'm certain nobody did that; if anything, I was afraid even to touch her little foot because she screamed whenever anyone so much as laid a finger on it. I remembered too that both Monday and Tuesday night she had cried a lot with the pain, but on Wednesday morning, before they took her for the operation, she was quite calm, and even touched the foot herself.

At four the same afternoon, the clinical record indicates that Grecia's temperature was normal. The inflammation continued to decrease, and although there was still some bleeding, the dressings did not smell bad. As a precaution, antibiotic treatment continued, and the doctors decided to dress the foot every two days until they could operate to set the fractures. Although the gangrene had disappeared, the toes were still fractured and hence deprived of blood circulation, with high risk of necrosis of the bones.

Grecia was kept in the hospital until she could recover from anemia caused by the considerable loss of blood and for repair of the fractures. For various reasons, however, that procedure continued to be delayed, and it was never performed. Sometimes it happened that the patient had not been properly prepared for the operation; at other times it was because the operating room was occupied. At any rate, on March 12, Grecia was declared completely cured. The fractured toes had mended without complications, and she had totally regained the use of her foot.

Clinical evaluation

As we have seen, the bicycle accident resulted in both a gangrenous infection and two fractured toes. The fractures meant that the bones would normally be deprived of blood circulation, with the consequent danger of necrosis.

In the judgment of a trauma specialist who was consulted by the Postulation, reversal of the gangrenous process cannot have an exclusively natural explanation, bearing in mind how sudden it was. Three facts certify the presence of a serious form of gangrene: (1) The trauma was severe, as it is not easy to fracture the toes of a young child, whose bones are still quite supple; (2) the clinical manifestations were very serious—high fever, intense pain, anemia—as was the physical examination of the wound, which presented the characteristic symptoms of gangrene; (3) the decision to amputate was reached by joint agreement of several physicians and confirmed after consulting the plastic surgery department. This was not a hasty decision but one fully justified by the rapid development of the infection.

A specialist who made a careful study of the entire record reached the following judgment:

> This serious gangrene was *cured clinically* (sudden disappearance of the pain, the fever, the signs of inflammation, etc.); *radiographically* (it left no subsequent radiological deterioration; *completely* (without amputation of the foot or any substantial loss); *without any treatment* (apart from antibiotics, the girl was given no medication on the previous day and the fracture/dislocations had not been reduced); and *immediately* (on Tuesday she presented all the symptoms, while on Wednesday morning she had only

> partial loss of function). She was kept in the hospital's internal medicine department as a precautionary measure, given the intensity of what she had gone through.
>
> Having considered all these circumstances [the specialist wrote], I am of the opinion that from the medical point of view Grecia G.'s cure is inexplicable, and I can well understand the surprise of my colleagues who observed it at close quarters.

Grecia's mother cannot contain her joy and gratitude for this great favor. She has seen with her own eyes how God looks after all his children, regardless of skin color and social standing. "When they told me they were not going to operate," Rosa states, "I thought: 'God exists, God is great, and he has helped me.' Immediately I phoned Dr. M. and said to him, 'Doctor, Msgr. Escrivá has worked the miracle for me!' . . . And afterward I handed his little prayer card to everybody in the hospital, telling them how the Msgr. had helped me."

8. A Great Illumination

"Instantaneous recovery of sight after a pituitary tumor had caused secondary blindness." (March 1992)[13]

This story concerns a lay brother who has lived for many years in a contemplative monastery where he looks after the adjoining dairy. He had always enjoyed excellent health when, at the beginning of 1991, at age fifty-nine, he began to notice a progressive loss of the sense of taste, to the point where he was unable to distinguish the flavors of different foods. When this was quickly followed by the loss of his sense of smell, he asked for a medical consultation. Two specialists attributed the loss of both senses to a simple nasopharyngeal complaint. Giving no special importance to it, they prescribed no treatment.

By about the middle of the year 1991, a progressive and rapid loss of eyesight ensued. When it reached such an extreme that the lay brother could no longer count the grazing cows, he was forced to give up much of his work. In one of the reports he sent to the Postulation, the brother explains what was happening to him during those months:

> What type of life was I living during this illness? It remained the same as always, except that I could no longer read, even with special glasses for which I was fitted. All I could see were black spots. I still went to choir with the others and sang whatever I knew by heart, keeping quiet the rest of the time. In the dairy I could still give indications to the workers but was no longer able to help with the milking without bumping into things and knocking them over. . . .

A difficult diagnosis

The lay brother's blindness continued to advance. He tried using a telescope to keep track of the cows, but he soon gave

[13] The facts of this case are documented in *De fama signorum post beatificationem*, vol. 1, pp. 627–658.

that up. The loss of sight in both eyes was especially severe on the periphery; he could not make out objects to his left or right. At first there was still a narrow band of frontal vision, but it gradually narrowed. Within a short time all he could see were black spots.

In November 1991 he was taken to an ophthalmologist, who ruled out, after careful examination, any optical cause of blindness and advised him to consult a physician. Finally, in January 1992, he was admitted to a general hospital, where he underwent various examinations (X-rays of the base of the skull, a CAT scan, and nuclear magnetic resonance imaging [MRI]). These tests indicated the presence of a malignant brain tumor that was compressing the patient's optic chiasma, an x-shaped space located just centimeters behind the eyes, where optic nerves from each eye cross on their way to the brain.

When the patient was admitted to an oncological center, physicians made two attempts to take samples for a biopsy, acting on the assumption that a malignant tumor in the nasopharyngeal cavity was destroying the base of the cranium and infiltrating his sella turcica, a bony mass that partly surrounds the pituitary gland. Both attempts failed, due to the difficulty of accessing the diseased area. With the possibility of malignancy and invasion of the sella turcica, the patient was offered two possible courses of therapy: a surgical operation or irradiation of the base of the cranium and the sella turcica. He decisively rejected the first of these.

At this point the monastery's superior and infirmarian consulted a neurologist who was a good friend of the community. He thought the blindness could be caused, not by an invasive tumor at the base of the cranium, but by a benign hypophyseal tumor that was compressing the optic chiasma because of its excessive growth. If this presumption proved to be correct, it would be possible to treat the tumor with drugs.

A blood test taken on March 11 showed very high levels of prolactin, a hormone produced by the anterior lobe of the pituitary. This confirmed the hypothesis of the neurologist: very probably the tumor was secreting a pituitary fluid. The specialist prescribed a course of therapy consisting of bromocriptine, a drug used in treating nonoperable macro-adenomas and an alternative to surgery for patients with micro-adenomas. This treatment was scheduled to begin on March 26, 1992.

Invocation of Josemaría Escrivá

At that time the beatification of Msgr. Josemaría Escrivá in St. Peter's Square was less than two weeks away. Some of the media, instigated by a small pressure group, were spreading calumnies intended to block the beatification. Ecclesiastical officials who had taken part in the various stages of the Cause for Beatification were being accused of serious procedural irregularities. The resulting controversy was having repercussions even among religious communities.

The lay brother in this account was greatly saddened by these developments. Above all he sensed an unjustified lack of trust in the Church and the Holy Father. While he had never had contact with Opus Dei, he held it in esteem simply because the Church had approved it and because he had derived spiritual benefits earlier in his life from meditating on *The Way*, a book by Opus Dei's founder. He stated this in his first report (December 1992) several months after his cure. "Why did I commend myself to Msgr. Escrivá? Because as a boy I had read his book *The Way*. And also because I objected to the controversy over his beatification."

The cure took place during the night of March 26–27, 1992, just as the brother was beginning to take the prescribed medicine. When he retired to his cell to prepare for bed, he was pondering the controversy that was so troubling to him. He spoke inwardly to Josemaría Escrivá, as he explains:

> "If you restore my sight, I promise to notify the Cause for your Beatification." . . . It was a stormy Saturday night with much wind and rain. When it awakened me, I switched on the light, as usual, but now everything seemed very bright. I thought to myself: "The electric cables have come into contact and caused a great electrical intensity." But it wasn't that. It was my eyes, which had suddenly become

clear. From that moment on I've been able to see very well. I can even read a newspaper without glasses, and in choir I can see the small print plainly, even without glasses.

His cure from blindness was instantaneous, and it occurred immediately after he had invoked the intercession of Josemaría Escrivá. On the night of March 26 the lay brother was almost completely blind; the next morning he had fully recovered his sight. He went immediately to inform the infirmarian: "I said to him, 'Look, now I can see well, and I have no further need for medicine.' But he replied, 'No, it must be something psychological, and perhaps tomorrow you'll say you're completely blind again.' I said to him, 'No, I can see fine.' But in the end I obeyed and took the medicine."

At first, the lay brother did not want to tell anyone that he had invoked the intercession of the future Blessed Josemaría. He did not want to stir up more controversy in his community. Finally, several months later, at the end of 1992 and well past the beatification, he decided to speak up because, in his words, "my conscience was pricking me" for failing to mention the great favor he had received.

But let us return to the cure itself. The next day, when he told the infirmarian that he could see again, the brother also asked him to inform the specialist who knew his case. As may be supposed, the doctor's reaction was one of disbelief. As the brother recalls, he exclaimed, "No, no, that was never part of the plan; it must be the placebo effect of the pills."

In some illnesses, particularly psychosomatic ones, it is possible to explain some improvements by the placebo effect. But the lay brother's illness had an organic cause, of which there could be no doubt. Scientifically, then, it would be impossible for a placebo effect to be responsible for the instantaneous and complete remission of blindness caused by the compression of the optic chiasma.

Although he was convinced of his cure and fully aware of how it had occurred, the lay brother continued, out of obedience to his superiors, to accept the treatment prescribed. Three months later, CAT scans and magnetic resonance tests showed that the hypophyseal tumor had diminished by 75 percent. This was reaffirmed on November 30 by further tests. Five years after his cure, the brother continues to enjoy normal vision, with no sign of a relapse.

Clearly an occurrence of this kind has no natural explanation. A radiotherapist and a radiodiagnostician consulted by the Postulation stated, after detailed study of the case and careful examination of the brother, that his cure could not have resulted from medication, which had only been started the previous day. "Such a spectacular regression of the prolactinoma in such a short time (less than 24 hours) cannot be attributed solely to the use of bromocriptine (DCI), since the patient took only a third of an ounce. This dose is clearly disproportionate to the actual outcome." Though in full agreement with the prescribed course of therapy, the specialists cited the 75 percent reduction in the size of the tumor in less than three months: "Up to the present time, medical literature has not published any such spectacular regression and cure of a hypophyseal macro-adenoma."

As we have seen, the lay brother himself was never in doubt about what occurred: God heard his prayer through the intercession of the founder of Opus Dei. Like the man blind from birth whom Jesus cured (Jn 9: 1–41), the brother repeats over and over what actually happened (using third person in his testimony): "The recovery of his sight was not progressive and gradual, but all at once. When he went to bed on March 26 he could scarcely see anything, and when he got up the next day, he could see as well as he ever had." In his own voice he adds: "I . . . am moved when I speak about this. When I rise for matins every morning, I always pray that our Lord be glorified through Msgr. Escrivá. . . . Since he is a saint, we no longer pray *for* him. I ask that God may be glorified through him, and that the Church may be honored and edified. To me, Msgr. Escrivá has done a great service for the Church."

9. No More Crutches

"Instantaneous cure of a disability resulting from a broken tibia." (May 17, 1992) [14]

In Cerdanyola del Valles, a village near Barcelona, Spain, everyone knew Josep Más,[15] who was seventy at the time of this story. He had lived there in a small house since 1981, when he suddenly lost his job as a salesman due to the closing of his company. He was especially well known after a serious accident in 1982 left him crippled and unable to get around without crutches. According to the disability certificate issued in May 1983 and confirmed by physicians in November 1983 and June 1984, Josep was incapacitated "for any [kind of work] requiring mobility."

One of the villagers recalls that for several years he often saw Josep at the eight o'clock daily Mass in the parish church. He described him as "a man over sixty, who walked like a real invalid. He used to sit up front on the left side of the aisle; he walked with great difficulty, making a lot of noise with his crutches. Because of this," the witness continues, "he would be the last one in line for Communion and would return slowly to his seat."

For ten years, from 1982 to 1992, this was a familiar scene in his parish church. Then one day there was a dramatic change. The same witness continues: "On May 20, 1992, at the eight o'clock Mass . . . the priest, Father José Rosell, said in these or similar words: 'Let us give thanks for the strange cure of our friend Josep, who has come to Mass without his crutches.' Indeed, to my great surprise I saw that the man who had been crippled was no longer using crutches and was moving quite

[14] The facts of this case are documented en *De fama signorum post beatification*, vol. 1, pp. 151–310.

[15] In this account we give the full name of the person cured, as the whole case is publicly known. Josep was interviewed on many occasions by print and broadcast journalists. The event was reported not only in local newspapers but in the larger Spanish newspapers (from *El Pais* to *ABC* and *Diario 16*), and accounts appeared also in *La Stampa*, *L'Unità*, and *Il Popolo* in Italy.

normally." Josep's sudden cure was equally surprising to everyone else in Cerdanyola, beginning with the parish priest; as pastor of a fairly small community, Father José knew his flock very well.

What had happened during those days in May 1992 for Josep suddenly and completely to recover after ten years his ability to walk normally?

Two accidents with serious consequences

The central figure of this story is a devout Catholic who had led a very active life. He had held a number of jobs, such as electrician, cab driver, and salesman—all of them requiring a good deal of travel. He was out selling household appliances one day in 1966 when he got into a bad traffic accident. When he recovered consciousness he felt what was to be a permanent pain in the lower back. Occasionally an acute attack required therapy in order for him to continue working. A doctor he consulted told him that in time the pain would probably spread to his legs. The diagnosis was lumbar spondylitis.

Sixteen years later, another accident resulted in an even worse setback. On May 10, 1982, Josep was returning home by train from Barcelona when he suffered an apparently minor accident that was to leave him completely disabled. Here is his account: "To get home from the station I had to walk through a vacant field. It was about six in the evening when two big dogs came running at me, jumped up, and knocked me down. I lay there unconscious until policemen came upon me and administered first aid."

The police had been summoned by several bystanders who saw the incident. Josep was taken to a hospital in the nearby town of Sabadell; the preliminary diagnosis was cerebral concussion with associated mental confusion. As the doctors had not been advised of the cause, they took it to be a cerebrovascular insufficiency. A few hours later, more thorough examination revealed a fracture of the left lateral tibial plateau. A tight band was wrapped around the lower part of the affected leg and later replaced by an elastic knee bandage. Eleven days later Josep began rehabilitation.

Specialists familiar with such fractures realize that depression of the tibial plateau and opening of the epiphysis, even if properly treated, can seriously reduce a patient's mobility. A recent study shows that 70 percent of these fractures lead to instability due to displacement of the bone and accompanying damage to the kneecap and ligaments. Another study found that a deviation of only a third of an inch from the axis leads to a lateral deviation of the tibia ("valgus", or knock-knee in common language), which can be corrected by adequate treatment in 60 percent of the cases. Unfortunately, Josep did not receive expert treatment. One of his sisters states that after the accident she was surprised that Josep was discharged without a cast. When she protested, she was told that nothing further was needed " . . . because with a fracture of that kind he would be crippled and unable to walk normally again."

Josep adds: "When I left the hospital with that double handicap—the old one in my back and the new one in my knee—I was told to get crutches and receive rehabilitation. I recall being told that if I didn't use the crutches I wouldn't be able to walk; and besides, they would keep me from putting my whole weight on the injured leg. When I told them I wanted to go back to work, they said that the injury was untreatable and my working days were over. I was given a document certifying that I would never be able to work again."

Josep attended rehabilitation sessions for the next four years. As he was practically unable to walk, even with the crutches, Social Security provided an ambulance for these trips. He continued to live alone, but his sister and a niece came to look after him. "During those four years," Josep recalls,

> I couldn't go to Mass. I never left the house except in the ambulance, and the parish priest brought me Holy Communion whenever he could.
>
> After that I discontinued the rehabilitation because there was so little improvement. . . . One of my sisters suggested that I have the little van I had used for work adapted for handicapped driving. This was done, and in spite of the

pain in my back and the immobility of my leg, being able to get around cheered me up a lot.

During all those years I was never without the crutches except at home; my house was small enough to get around in by holding onto furniture, walls, or shelves. In spite of the care I was receiving, I gradually started to feel worse. As the pain increased, I considered returning to the doctor to see if he could recommend any other treatment, such as a new medication that might have become available.

The moment of the cure

As the years passed, Josep continually asked God to heal him. In May he would invoke our Lady and in June the Sacred Heart of Jesus. In the other months he appealed to several intercessors to whom he was devoted—some of them saints and others who had died with a reputation for holiness. He never got discouraged, even if his prayers seemed to go unheard.

He did not hear of Msgr. Escrivá until the end of April or beginning of May 1992. It may have been on April 27, the feast of Our Lady of Montserrat, or on May 1, which was the First Friday that year (he cannot recall for sure), when a young man handed him a prayer card as he was coming out of church. "I didn't remember ever having seen that boy before, but he must have seen me at Mass at other times, since disabled persons always attract attention." Josep thanked him for the card, but when he got back home he didn't give it much importance: "That day," he says, "I only said the prayer once."

The beatification of Opus Dei's founder was approaching and was frequently mentioned in the news media. On Friday, May 15, Josep learned by way of television that the beatification would take place the following Sunday, the 17th. As he had not realized it was so close, this report seemed to him a summons. Here is his account of the events of that day:

On Sunday, May 17, I went to Mass as usual at the parish church. When I got back home I turned on the television,

> thinking that the ceremony might be televised since such a large number of people had gone to it—more than two hundred thousand, as they had been reporting. . . .

Josep's antenna, however, was unable to pick up the channel on which the live telecast from St. Peter's Square was being shown.

> After having breakfast, I went out to clean the hen house. At about eleven, I thought, "The beatification must be taking place about now. So I said to the Venerable Servant of God, 'If you're going to heal me, this has to be the day because we're in the month of Mary and I'm praying to Our Lady of Montserrat. Since today's the day they're beatifying you, if you heal me today it'll have to be attributed to you.' " Then I said the Rosary, the prayer for private devotion, and the Our Father. As soon as I'd finished I realized that the pain I used to have constantly, for which I had to take aspirins or other analgesics (even if they didn't really help that much), had disappeared. It was quite sudden. I also realized that I could move around much more easily. Then I said to Blessed Josemaría, as he was by that time, "Now I'll do a novena in your honor," which I began there and then so that it would end on May 25. Then I decided that on the 25th itself, if I really was healed, I'd go to [the hospital] for an X-ray.

The next day Josep stayed home, still feeling no pain and taking no pain relievers, but wondering how to explain to people what had happened.

On May 19 he went shopping. "As usual, I took the car, with its handicapped plates, and parked in the reserved space. I got out of the car and, I don't know how, but as soon as I was on the pavement I lifted up the crutches and said to myself, 'I can walk!' That's when I realized that Blessed Josemaría really had completely healed me, and I said to myself, 'Tomorrow I've got to go to Mass to say thank you!' "

The pastor saw Josep arrive:

I saw him coming toward the church that morning on the 20th of last May, and it struck me because the Josep Más I had known up until then was disabled.... When I saw him coming in without crutches I was really astonished; I couldn't figure out how this could be possible. My reaction was one of enormous surprise. After ten years of always seeing him on crutches, there he was before my eyes without them and walking normally, with no difficulty at all. I was amazed and perplexed. I even wondered if it really was Josep, but there could be no doubt. When I asked him what had happened, the first thing he said was, "That man in Rome...." I realized right away that he was talking about the newly beatified Josemaría Escrivá.

He entered the Blessed Sacrament chapel, where the Mass was to be celebrated. Quite a number of people were there, and before Mass ended I felt I had to say a few words: "We have all seen Mr. Josep Más on crutches for the last ten years and now we see him walking without crutches. This is a lovely surprise for me, and I thank God, because it is unquestionably a gift from the Lord."

After Mass [the priest continues], he came into the sacristy and told me that the pains in his back and leg had disappeared. "I can stand up without crutches... and it seems really strange to me." As he spoke, he dropped to his knees and got up again as if on springs. My surprise continued to grow because of the contrast between what I had seen for so many years and what I was seeing at that moment."

A permanent cure

The news of this sudden cure reached the media at once, and it was reported in the newspapers, on the radio, and on television. The Town Council named Josep "Man of the Year."

He was so completely convinced that he had received an extraordinary grace that he did not hesitate to undergo clinical examinations, X-rays, and psychological testing, so that the reality of what had happened could be proved scientifically.

On May 23, 1992, a physician examined him and confirmed that he had been healed. Josep was described as "well-oriented in space and time; he walks without needing crutches and without limping; he can bend his leg, kneel down, and get up without support, and has normal mobility of the spine." In a written statement several months later, the same doctor added: "I had an opportunity to speak to the heads of rehabilitation centers at Cerdanyola and Sabadell, which Josep frequented between 1982 and 1984. They remembered him as a disabled man who walked on crutches and always came in an ambulance and who discontinued the rehabilitation because it wasn't helping him to improve."

In July 1992 Josep was seen by a specialist in traumatology and orthopedics, whose report notes the absence of any pain in the spine and knee, normal mobility for a man of his age, osteoarthritic lesions in the cervical and lumbar regions of the spinal column, and severe damage to the disk joints in the lumbo-sacral region—the result of a former fracture of the outer tibial plane, with few degenerative consequences. It is not, therefore, an anatomical cure, since X-rays previous to May 17 and afterward are the same; rather, it is a functional cure all the more surprising because the cause of the disability from which Josep had suffered for ten years still remained. This leads the specialist to conclude: "We find it surprising, given the clinical profile on the patient's record and the reports dating from 1982 onward which he still retains, that he is now free of pain and fully able to walk normally without crutches."

A year and a half later the situation remained stable. In response to a request from the Postulation, a professor of orthopedic surgery and traumatology at the Autonomous University of Barcelona gave Josep another check-up and confirmed his complete functional normality of movement, noting in his report the same radiological pathology as was given previously. A psychological examination at the end of 1993 continued to show no behavioral abnormality.

The Postulation also submitted the case record to three Italian specialists. A professor of legal medicine at the University of Naples writes: "Complete functional recovery after ten years of using crutches is inexplicable in the present state of our knowledge, both because of its suddenness and because there are no therapeutic resources capable of correcting such long-established symptoms. For purposes of a medical-legal judgment, the fact that the local anatomical defects persist is not relevant, because the functional defect has completely ceased."

This conclusion, which confirms the scientifically inexplicable nature of Josep Más's recovery, is particularly important because the specialist who wrote it, who has since died, was a member of the medical commission of the Congregation for the Causes of Saints and was therefore very familiar with the criteria governing medical-legal judgments of alleged cures. For that commission, proof of a functional cure is sufficient to describe it as inexplicable by natural causes, even without a *restitutio ad integrum* (anatomical cure).

A Roman traumatologist, after a thorough examination of the X-rays, states: "In such cases, a patient's condition naturally develops toward progressive deterioration, or, in the very best cases and with suitable treatment, a slow, gradual and always provisional diminishing of the symptoms. . . . Thus a spontaneous and immediate remission of pain and functional incapacity, such as occurred in the case of Josep Más, is inexplicable, given the type of fracture and the ten-year duration of the disability, which was clinically and medically certified."

Finally, another doctor, also a member of the Congregation's medical commission, concludes:

> I must emphasize one fundamental and essential fact, which is that the severe pain and incapacitating functional disability ceased suddenly, while the anatomical lesions persisted. By no means could this be accounted for by simulation on the part of the patient, who for many years suffered such a serious disability that it not only prevented him from working, but even from maintaining the most basic social contacts. The persistence of anatomical lesions does not in any way invalidate the judgment that the

> cure is scientifically inexplicable, since in my opinion the most important fact in this case is the cessation . . . of the disability."

* * *

Four years after the events related here, Josep Más, in spite of his age (seventy-five), was still perfectly mobile. After this period of time it can safely be stated that the functional cure of his disability was instantaneous, complete, and permanent. Accordingly, the judgment of all the medical experts is that "the cure was inexplicable *quoad modum* [because of the manner in which it took place]."

10. A Mother's Faith

"Instantaneous cure of a serious case of high blood pressure due to a defective renal artery." (May 17, 1992)[16]

Some extraordinary graces have remarkable parallels in the Gospel. The following account recalls a cure Jesus performed in answer to a father's plea on behalf of his son who was suffering from violent convulsions (Mark 9: 14-29). After the Transfiguration on Mount Tabor, Jesus came down to the plain and found his disciples in a crowd of people as they tried to cure a young boy who was in a desperate state, due (as St. Mark informs us) to an evil spirit. Since the apostles were apparently helpless against it, the boy's father begged Jesus to cure him.

"How long has he been like this?" asked our Lord, and the father answered, "Since childhood. It has often cast him into fire and into water, to destroy him; but if you can do anything, have pity on us and help us." Jesus replied, "If *you* can! All things are possible to him who believes." Fearful that a lack of faith might prevent his son from being cured, the boy's father fell at the Lord's feet, exclaiming, "I believe; help my unbelief!" Moved by this wonderful act of faith, the Lord cured the boy and gave him back to his father.

While the circumstances are different, this miracle is reflected in the following cure attributed to the intercession of Blessed Josemaría Escrivá. One common feature stands out. In the Gospel account, an anguished father's cry of faith touched

[16] The facts of this case are documented in *De fama signorum post beatificationem*, vol. 1, pp. 9–147. A diocesan investigation was held into this cure at the Archdiocesan Curia of Oviedo, Spain, from March 28 to October 11, 1995. In the course of fourteen sessions, ten witnesses were examined, including well-known nephrological specialists and university professors, who described and confirmed the cure. The documentation includes the child's complete clinical history and several studies of the case. The experts appointed by the diocesan tribunal verified that the cure was perfect, complete, and permanent. The minutes of the investigation are recorded in a three-volume document entitled *Procedures*.

the heart of Jesus; in the present case, an anguished mother's cry, also springing from deep faith, obtained from God a humanly inexplicable cure.

An unexpected discovery

In October 1985, the marriage of Manuel Vicente A. and María Josefa M. was crowned with happiness by the birth of their first son. The baby boy was born in Oviedo, a city in the Asturias region of northern Spain, and given the name Manuel Adrián.

The first years of his life passed normally, and he was growing up in a home full of love. Six years later, in 1991, he was joined by twin brothers. Everything had gone well until the beginning of 1988, when Manuel Adrián, not yet three, began to suffer frequent attacks of dysnea, or breathing difficulties, which occurred along with minor infections and colds. The doctor diagnosed asthma.

Almost a year later he was rushed to the hospital with intense abdominal pains, to be operated on for acute appendicitis. This, however, was not the worst of it; in the preliminary examination, a severe hypertensive blood pressure was discovered with readings of up to 220/140. To appreciate the seriousness of Manuel Adrián's condition, one should consider that the blood pressure of children is lower than for adults, and that a reading of 140/80 is already borderline in adults.

An effort was made to reduce the pressure by means of an intravenous treatment with sodium nitroprusside, used only in very severe cases where there is danger of cerebral hemorrhage or imminent death. This brought the pressure down sufficiently to operate on the appendix, which was becoming worse by the hour and increasing the danger of peritonitis. Examination of the appendix during the operation showed typical signs of inflammation, perforation, and incipient gangrene. During the operation and for the next three days the little patient suffered a hypertensive crisis on several occasions, with readings as high as 230/140.

A serious, incurable, progressive disease

Once the appendix was removed and the blood pressure came down, the doctors concentrated on identifying the underlying cause. Manuel Adrián was moved to pediatric nephrology, where a team of experts using special equipment conducted a series of tests that excluded the most common causes of high blood pressure in children. After an abdominal arteriogram, the cause of the hypertension was provisionally diagnosed as renal artery stenosis. Since this is incurable, only the symptoms could be treated, by using drugs to keep the blood pressure normal. The parents were advised to take the child's blood pressure frequently.

Manuel Adrián went back home, but between February and December of the same year (1989) he was rushed to the hospital in critical condition on four occasions when attacks of asthma or minor infections common in early childhood raised his blood pressure to dangerous levels. This was only the beginning of an agonizing vigil for Manuel Vicente and María Josefa, distraught at the thought of losing their only son in one of these attacks.

At the beginning of 1990, a year after the appendicitis, they took him to Madrid for confirmation of the diagnosis. During a month of examinations at the Ramon y Cajal Hospital, the recurring bouts with high blood pressure were traced to "intra-renal stenosis of the right renal artery, not suitable for dilation or surgical operation." As the patient was so young it was thought that the stenosis was due to fibromuscular dysplasia, an anomaly in the development of the arterial wall.

This confirmed that Manuel Adrián's infirmity was incurable. All that could be done was to treat the symptoms and hope for the best from month to month. Over the long term, this condition ordinarily leads to early fatality because it tends to cause irremediable lesions in vital organs such as the brain, heart, and kidneys. Moreover, the hypertension which it causes, as described in medical literature, leads to a progressive increase in the obstruction of the affected artery, particularly during early childhood. This is what occurred in all forty-two patients with narrowing of the renal artery caused by fibromuscular dysplasia who were studied over an eleven-year period by a medical team, as reported in an international journal of high repute. The diagnosis in the present case was further confirmed by a specific test that can precisely differentiate hypertension of reno-vascular origin from all other forms of hypertensive disease.

Clinical research shows that this kind of high blood pressure might be circumvented through by-pass surgery to replace the defective section of the artery or by doing a kidney transplant. In Manuel Adrián's case this was deemed to be inadvisable. The only recourse was to control the hypertension by means of drugs. Once its cause was definitively identified, doctors prescribed Captopril, a treatment specific to reno-vascular hypertension, at eight-hour intervals. With this dismal prospect for his future, the child was discharged.

Taking refuge in God

Under these circumstances, Manuel Adrián's mother turned to God. "In desperation, I sought refuge and consolation in God, and suddenly I remembered the little card with Monsignor's prayer on it," she said. "Someone had given it to me the first time my child took ill, and I had put it away without paying it the slightest attention." The little boy's parents were practicing Catholics, but not particularly fervent, as they themselves explain in a letter to the Opus Dei Vice-postulation Office in Spain on June 1, 1992, reporting the favor they had received through Msgr. Escrivá's intercession: "Although we are believers, we are not model Catholics—far from it, and to be honest, we must admit that Opus Dei was quite distant from our thoughts, that it meant nothing to us at all." But what Christian mother with an only son seriously ill does not appeal to God's mercy with faith? This is what María Josefa did, beseeching our Lord through the intercession of the founder of Opus Dei, who at that time had not yet been beatified.

A sister-in-law had given her the prayer card in 1989 when Manuel Adrián underwent the appendectomy. Her words were: "Just ask him." But it was not until a time of deep anguish, several months later, that María Josefa followed her advice. This was at the end of September 1990, during one of the child's frequent bouts with a sudden rise in blood pressure following an asthma attack. Such an attack is frightening to witness. As the person gasps for breath, the pulse races, with the heart trying uselessly to send more blood to the lungs. Labored breathing gives way to wheezing; the person breaks out in a cold sweat, and the skin turns a bluish color, especially the hands and feet. In the case of a small child, these symptoms are even more distressing. One can readily imagine how much all this must cause the parents to suffer helplessly as they anticipate possible consequences of the excessively high blood pressure that will ensue.

This is why María Josefa finally turned to Msgr. Escrivá, begging him to intercede with our Lord on behalf of her son: "I began to pray it [the prayer on the card] with blind faith, convinced that it was the only thing that could cure my son." First she prayed that the asthma attacks would stop. This prayer was answered immediately, for on October 2, 1990, once he had recovered from the asthmatic bronchitis for which he had been taken to the hospital, the boy was able to go home. "From that moment on," his mother states, "he never had another asthma attack. . . . He never needed to be given oxygen again, or even be hospitalized."

As time passed and she realized that the asthma had been cured, María Josefa's faith in God and confidence in Msgr. Escrivá's intercession became stronger: "I grew bolder, and prayed for him to be cured little by little of this treacherous illness." Her reason for asking by stages rather than for a complete cure all at once was related to an ecclesiastical tribunal in Oviedo: "I prayed for him to be cured of his high blood pressure, but little by little. Given the medication he was taking, I feared that a sudden cure might make his blood pressure drop too quickly and cause his death."

By summer's end 1991, María Josefa was also asking others to join in her pleas to Msgr. Escrivá by sending them prayer cards. Around that time Manuel Adrián's condition took a new turn. He began to experience slight dizziness on getting up in the morning, a probable symptom of low blood pressure induced by the drug. When his mother noticed this, she informed the doctors, who summoned him for a series of checkups; the medication was reduced to keep pace with a progressive decline in the blood pressure. Between November 1991 and April 1992 the daily dosage went down from 32 to 13 milligrams.

At a precise moment

On May 17, 1992, the day Msgr. Escrivá was beatified in Rome, Manuel Adrián was seven. That Sunday was a hot, sunny day in Oviedo, and his father took him to the beach while his mother stayed home with his twin baby brothers, born a year earlier. María Josefa's statement to the tribunal in Oviedo relates the events of that day:

> On May 17 my husband went to the beach with Adrián (it was a hot day), while I stayed home with the twins. I turned on the television to watch the ceremony of what I thought at the time was the "sanctification" of the Servant of God Josemaría Escrivá, since I wasn't able to distinguish sanctification from beatification. At a precise moment in the ceremony, as I held the prayer card in my hands, I closed my eyes, my mind seemed to go blank, and I begged Josemaría Escrivá to intercede for my child's complete cure. With my eyes still closed, I could see him smiling at me. That gave me the total, absolute certainty that he was granting me the favor I was asking for. When the liturgical celebration was over I was fully convinced, completely and absolutely certain that he had heard my prayer and that my son had been cured.
>
> When my husband returned in the afternoon, he told me that while they were on the beach Manuel Adrián had started to feel cold, although it was a very warm day, and so he had covered him with towels. When the child awoke from a little nap, he told his father that he was feeling very well. I asked my husband what time this had happened; I don't now remember what time it was, but it was at the

same time that I was praying to God through Josemaría Escrivá's intercession. My husband was really moved.

Immediately, María Josefa took the boy's blood pressure (after so long she was an expert at it) and found it to be perfectly normal. Next day she took him to the hospital, although he was not due for another examination until October. "Something inside me," she says, "was telling me that the boy was cured, and it was true; they stopped his medication, and he's fine."

Several specialists in nephrology and endocrinology have carefully studied the case. According to Professor Jesús B., professor of nephrology at the University of Valladolid, "The disappearance of high blood pressure without medical or surgical treatment in a case of reno-vascular hypertension well confirmed by testing with Captopril treatment and by conventional arteriography is not, medically speaking, understandable." Professor Manuel de S., head of endocrinology at a well-known hospital in Madrid, reached the same conclusion when testifying during the investigation of the alleged miracle in the diocese of Oviedo:

> Medical opinion is unanimous that reno-vascular hypertension does not resolve spontaneously. That means that it is incurable, short of a surgical operation or the use of techniques closely allied to surgery. . . . In such cases the opinion of the medical profession is that there is no spontaneous regression of the condition causing vascular stenosis, the mechanism leading to the development of arterial hypertension. . . . I only wish to add quite simply that the cure of hypertension that took place in this child, in view of the diagnoses that had been made and to which I subscribe, seems to me medically inexplicable; it cannot be interpreted scientifically.

The conclusion of these specialists, after careful study of the relevant literature, is unanimous: There is no natural explanation of how Manuel Adrián's blood pressure could be completely normal after he stopped taking the drug that, for almost three years, had been used to control it. Nor were there any recurrences of the acute hypertensive crises with common childhood ailments like sore throats or colds subsequent to the cure. The cure has no scientific explanation. It was decided not to attempt a proof of the normality of the defective renal artery in this case because a new arteriogram would have been necessary, and due to their son's age and the normal state of his health, his parents decided against such an invasive test. Whether or not the narrowing of the artery persists is irrelevant to the validity of the medical judgment that the child's cure is impossible to explain naturally.

* * *

More than five years have passed, and Manuel Adrián still leads a normal life. He has almost no recollection of those early years when he was in serious danger. His parents, however, have certainly not forgotten, and they thank God every day for the huge favor he granted to them through the intercession of Blessed Josemaría Escrivá.

11. Vanished without a Trace

"Disappearance of a large para-uterine cyst in a pregnant woman." (September 1992)[17]

Maria Grazia L. and Claudio P., recently married, set out with high hopes to cooperate with God in forming a Christian family. A few months after the wedding, in June 1991, their first child was on the way. This was a joyful incentive in hastening their efforts to find a more suitable place to live. As they canvassed several neighborhoods in Rome, they discovered that the prices were far beyond reach. The only solution, they thought, and "the only weapon at our command, was to put the matter in the hands of the founder of the Work, and rely on him to find the place where we should begin to carry out our matrimonial vocation."

No sooner said than done. They started a novena to Josemaría Escrivá, whom the Church was to beatify a few months later. On the seventh day they signed the contract to buy a house that would meet all their needs. This filled Maria Grazia and Claudio with gratitude to God and strengthened their belief in the power of prayer and the intercession of the saints. But this grace was only the forerunner of a much greater favor a few months later, again through the intercession of Blessed Josemaría.

A cyst during the pregnancy

Maria's pregnancy followed a normal course. On March 10, ten weeks along, she went in for an ultrasound exploration. Alongside the fetus, which was normal, the scan showed a cyst probably originating from the ovaries or fallopian tubes. The gynecologist decided not to intervene at that stage so as not to risk damaging the fetus; the cyst would grow along with it, and by the eighth month an operation would reduce its size and make it possible to deliver by cesarean section.

[17] The details of this case are documented in *De fama signorum post beatificationem*, vol. 2, pp. 709–752.

Thereafter the cyst's development was monitored at intervals. Successive ultrasound explorations indicated that the gynecologist's predictions were correct. On March 30, three weeks after it was discovered, the cyst had grown to a diameter of three inches from front to back. When on August 20 the diameter had surpassed five inches, the gynecologist decided that it was no longer prudent to wait and obtained the couple's consent to aspirate the cyst five days later under ultrasound control, cesarean delivery to follow.

Surprise in the operating room

Things did not turn out as planned. On August 25, the operation began with a new ultrasound scan to guide the surgeon. The technician, however, much to everyone's astonishment, announced that the cyst had vanished without leaving a trace. "There is no trace of the cyst previously observed," his report stated. But as each exploration had shown, a cyst really had been present. Naturally, the operation was cancelled, and the pregnancy continued normally. A scan on September 3 confirmed the absence of a cyst. On September 24, Maria Grazia gave birth to Francesca in a normal delivery.

From a medical point of view the disappearance of such a large cyst, which had been observed and measured only five days previously, cannot be explained by merely natural causes. If the cyst had burst spontaneously—improbable but not impossible—it would have left detectable remains. But there was nothing to show that it had ever existed. Maria Grazia's gynecologist put it in explicit terms: "The ultrasound scan on August 25 showed the disappearance of a cyst that had been seen repeatedly over the preceding months. Neither was there a sign of any fluid in the peritoneal cavity or in the Douglas pouch. There were no signs of fluid accumulation or other symptoms then or in the following days." He concluded: "It would be entirely unique for a cyst to rupture without leaving any symptoms or signs and without any spilling of the cystic fluid into the peritoneal cavity, especially a cyst of this size, as large as a baby's head."

Since there is no natural explanation for such a singular

event, Maria Grazia and Claudio have no doubt that the sudden and complete disappearance of the cyst came about through the intercession of Blessed Josemaría, whom they had been invoking since the diagnosis was first made. They write: "We immediately and confidently turned to Blessed Josemaría, praying insistently for the best possible outcome for our child."

On August 25, when they were informed of the unexpected and inexplicable disappearance of the cyst and learned that there would be no operation, the couple took it as proof that their prayers had been answered. "We firmly believe that these extraordinary favors have been granted through the intervention of Blessed Josemaría Escrivá, to whom we still turn constantly, with childlike trust, in all our needs."

12. A Nightmare that Lasted Eleven Hours

"Inexplicable and complete recovery from cardiac arrest and resulting cerebral damage." (October 2, 1992)[18]

The following story is about an eighty-seven—year-old man, Luis C., who lived in Madrid with his wife. What is most remarkable about it is the brief space of time in which the events transpired. The entire episode—from an acute heart attack, prolonged cardiorespiratory arrest, and subsequent signs of brain damage, to complete recovery—took only eleven hours. It is likely more than a coincidence that it should have taken place during the night of October 1 to 2, anniversary of the inspiration to found Opus Dei, which Blessed Josemaría received from God in 1928.

Most of the medical evidence comes from the patient's son, Dr. Alberto C., a cardiologist, who attended to him from the first moment. Because of the urgency of the situation, it was impossible to bring the patient to a hospital where the usual resuscitation equipment would have been available. This circumstance makes it even more difficult to explain how an elderly man could recover so quickly from such a serious condition, and with no ill effects.

Like a bolt from the blue

Born in 1905, Luis was the father of eleven healthy children. He had rarely suffered infirmities prior to the heart attack in 1992. A duodenal ulcer was kept under control by simple antacids. At age seventy-nine a benign prostate tumor was successfully removed, and two years later he was successfully treated for an acute myocardial infarction. Since then he had enjoyed relatively good health for a man of his age. He never left home, and he made use of a wheelchair to get around. A porter in the building came every morning to help him get up and about. The attack on October 1, 1992, struck like a bolt from the blue.

[18] The details of this case are documented in *De fama signorum post beatificationem*, vol. 1, pp. 313–382.

That night, between 10:30 and 11 P.M., as the porter was helping Luis prepare for bed, his eyes suddenly rolled upward, his head dropped, breathing stopped, and he went completely limp. Very frightened, the porter immediately phoned the old man's son, Alberto, a cardiologist; fortunately, he and his wife were at home, entertaining guests. According to Alberto's wife, Isabel A., he immediately left the room with his friend Carlos M.

She continued:

> I stayed with Carlos' wife, and as we awaited news about my father-in-law, knowing how serious the situation was, I turned with great confidence to the prayer card of Blessed Josemaría Escrivá. I've always said that prayer whenever a problem arose, especially if it had to do with the children, my husband, or our domestic employees. That night I put my father-in-law's cure entirely in Blessed Josemaría's hands, as I suspected that no cure by ordinary human means was likely, given his age and the earlier heart attack."

A race against time

Alberto's complete and authoritative testimony tells the story of what happened that night: "I went immediately to the home of my parents, accompanied by Carlos, bringing with me only a stethoscope, a sphygmomanometer [an instrument for measuring arterial blood pressure] and emergency drugs. On the way we said the prayer for devotion to Blessed Josemaría Escrivá. Carlos pronounced the words slowly, and I united myself to them, asking God for what was best for my father." His spontaneous reaction to the crisis, like that of his wife, was to seek divine intervention.

One of Luis' daughters, Pilar C., lived in the same apartment building and was the first one to reach his bedside. She describes the scene:

> When we arrived, my father was lying unconscious in the wheelchair, supported by the porter, Sebastian. I felt for his

> pulse at the wrist and neck but couldn't detect anything. His face was completely drained of color, pupils dilated and mouth open. My husband helped Sebastian move him onto the bed. When they laid him down he made a noise as though expelling air, a sort of rasping sound, which we thought was an attempt to breathe, but it wasn't. I tried to find his pulse again but without success. As we covered him with a shawl to keep him warm, my brother, Alberto arrived.

Given Alberto's many years of experience, his statement is especially significant in describing his father's condition:

> Although we had set off immediately after my mother called, the attack had occurred between fifteen and twenty minutes before we got there. My father was lying on the bed, clearly in a state of cardiopulmonary arrest. He was unconscious, pale, and made no respiratory sound of any kind. I could only detect a slight reflex movement in the diaphragm. I tried the radial, femoral, and carotid pulses, but with negative results. As he gave no clinical signs of life for quite a long time, I simply assumed that my father had died. He was completely immobile; there was no respiration, no pulse, no audible heartbeat on auscultation [listening for sounds in the chest], the pupils were dilated, and his face was like a corpse. [This clinical description matches that of a dead person.] Clearly, one could not establish exactly when the cardiac arrest occurred, but I estimate at least fifteen to twenty minutes before my arrival; I can be certain that it took us only six or eight minutes to get to him.

The time factor is obviously decisive in such a case with respect to the possibility of reviving vital functions. Scientific studies have shown that the key to a successful recovery is maintenance of cardiopulmonary functions and optimum oxygenation of vital organs. Normally this would be achieved by means of basic and advanced life-support techniques. According to a specialist in resuscitation who studied the case at the

Postulation's request, "The prospect for surviving cardiac arrest is greatly improved if basic resuscitation can be started within the first four minutes, and advanced heart-and-lung resuscitation within the first eight minutes. This applies primarily to those cases associated with ventricular fibrillation [irregular heartbeat]"—which he thought the most probable cause of cardiac arrest in this case. The first medical assistance, however, was administered, according to Alberto's estimate, beyond that time frame. The specialist concluded: "I estimate the cardiac arrest to have occurred shortly before the arrival of his son; since it is apparent that this exceeded the four to six minutes previously mentioned, and given the circumstances of the patient (no hypothermia, age, previous pathology, and so on), I find his recovery inexplicable both because of the time elapsed and because of the scanty therapeutic resources available."

A humanly inexplicable recovery

Although clinical symptoms indicated that Luis was already dead, his son used all available means to sustain whatever life might be present. Having nothing more than simple instruments for listening to the heart and measuring blood pressure, Alberto had to rely on external cardiac massage, which he began immediately. This would be the instinctive reaction of any doctor confronted with cardiac arrest. But normally this measure can succeed only within the first few moments. That time had elapsed, as we have seen, when Alberto began the procedure.

"But within five minutes of starting the massage," he continues, "I noticed some cardiac movement, and the pulse reappeared; it was very rapid. Respiratory movements were very slow." It seemed as if the patient was reviving. But then "he immediately started to exhibit myoclonic movements with hyperextension and internal rotation of the upper extremities, indicative of cerebral ischaemia [blood deficiency, or local anemia]. These movements were manifest and persistent."

Alberto realized that his father's behavior indicated that the brain cells, deprived for too long of blood, were showing signs of irreversible damage. The others also realized this, as Pilar recalls: "Alberto asked us to leave the room because my father was showing signs of 'decerebrement' or 'decerebration'—I can't recall which [i.e., deterioration of mental activity]. His body was quite stiff, and his hands were twisted back. I went to another room with my mother and my son Carlos."

Alberto's friend Carlos M. reports the same experience. He had been dispatched to an all-night pharmacy for medication. "I was away for about ten minutes on this errand, and when I returned, Alberto's father, still unconscious, was beginning to breathe again, in a very labored way, noisily and irregularly. He was frothing at the mouth. Alberto expressed consternation as he told me, 'If he comes out of this he'll be in terrible shape because his brain has been without oxygen for so long.' He pointed to his father's twisted hands as a sign of brain damage."

Although the cardiac massage had brought Luis out of arrest, indications of brain damage resulted in a very poor prognosis. After reviewing the case, the resuscitation specialist mentioned earlier came to these conclusions: Poor prognosis takes into account (1) the patient's age; (2) signs of brain damage (convulsions but, above all, the evidence of decerebration, such as abnormal extension and internal rotation of the upper limbs); (3) the initial level of consciousness as measured on the Glasgow coma scale was less than seven; (4) the suboptimal means of resuscitation used. The same specialist explained that many studies have shown how accurate the Glasgow scale is in forming a prognosis. With an initial figure of seven, half of the patients die or remain in a persistent vegetative state; if the figure is three or four, the rate of mortality rises to about 90 percent.

A silent cry

The family's petitions for Blessed Josemaría's intercession continued all night. The priest of a nearby parish came to anoint Luis and confer the Sacrament of the Sick. As we have seen, Alberto's greatest concern was that if his father survived, he could remain in a permanent vegetative state:

"Aware of the gravity of his situation, I administered Fraxipana and Valium subcutaneously. The former is an anticoagulant used in cases of thrombosis, the latter a relaxant acting centrally to lessen convulsions. . . . I was almost sorry I had given the massage when I saw my father in this state. I implored God, through the intercession of Blessed Josemaría, for his heart to stop again, or for him to recover completely." It was a silent cry, straight from a son's heart. At that point Luis was in a coma, and the pulse was very rapid. Alberto remained at his bedside throughout the night, administering appropriate medication.

About eleven hours after the heart attack, Luis suddenly and unexpectedly awoke from the coma; it was 10 A.M. on October 2. There was rapid improvement in his alertness, and within a few minutes he was perfectly lucid. Half an hour later his son made an electrocardiogram. To his complete astonishment, Alberto could not detect any sign of the cardiac arrest. The only abnormality was the presence of Q waves, the result of the infarction he had suffered in 1986, which had also appeared on earlier tracings. Blood tests were made, and all the hematological and biochemical values were within normal ranges. Within a few hours Luis had recovered sufficiently to perform simple calculations. The nightmare had ended.

"I cannot explain what happened that night, October 1 to 2, 1992," Alberto admits.

> In my opinion it was an extraordinary event for which there is no natural explanation. I have never seen such a case of complete recovery. Judging from my professional experience, which is wide and varied enough, so rapid and complete a recovery from the haemodynamic and neurological effects of cardiac arrest cannot be explained by natural causes. I know of no case similar to this one. For me it is an extraordinary cure, which Blessed Josemaría Escrivá de Balaguer obtained from the Lord.

Following his remarkable recovery, Luis led a normal, healthy life, considering his advanced age. He died January 22,

1995, just before his ninetieth birthday. "Over a period of several months," Alberto adds, "he became progressively more agile than he had been before the cardiac arrest. He was even able to get around the apartment without needing his wheelchair." Isabel, his daughter-in-law and Alberto's wife, made the same observation in November 1993, more than a year later: "Before he 'died' on that night of October 1, 1992, he never went out and could get around only in a wheelchair. . . . Since then he's been walking normally and looking after his own personal needs." She continues: "A few days ago my mother-in-law briefly summarized the situation: 'Since his resuscitation he's been much better, better than he was before it happened.' This simple statement says it all."

13. A Complete Restoration

"Sudden recovery of sensation and movement in a student's hand." (February 1993)[19]

Luis Fernando R., a sixteen-year-old student at Intisana, a high school conducted by Opus Dei in Quito, Ecuador, had always enjoyed good health until one day at school he suffered a serious accident. It is common for high-spirited youths to injure themselves, but what happened to Luis Fernando that day could have maimed him for life. Thanks to Blessed Josemaría Escrivá's intercession, however, everything turned out well for him.

A fall with serious consequences

On February 10, 1993, Luis Fernando was "letting off steam" following a chemistry test; as he sped down a corridor, his feet slipped out from under him. In an effort to keep from falling, he reached out for the frame of an open window and in the process accidentally broke the glass; a large sliver passed into his right hand. In an interview with the school paper, he described the result: "My hand was cut to the bone. The main nerve was severed, and so were the upper tendon and flexor tendon of my thumb. Altogether, five tendons were cut through, so my hand was only held on by the bone, which itself was cracked." This description is clear enough to indicate the severity of his injury. When he put his outstretched hand through the window, a shard of glass penetrated it like the blade of a knife, cutting everything in its path until halted by the bone.

Fortunately, the school doctor was on duty and able to give Luis Fernando first aid; to stem the flow of blood, Dr. Fernando M. applied a tourniquet to the arm and then took him to the emergency room of Quito's municipal hospital. "On the way," Luis Fernando recalls, "I was trying to see which fingers I could move. There was hardly any response from the thumb and

[19] The details of this case are documented in *De fama signorum post beatificationem*, vol. 2, pp. 673–707.

first two fingers and no feeling at all in them. The other two fingers were normal as regards movement and feeling. I didn't feel any pain, but I was still bleeding heavily. I started to feel pain about twenty minutes after the accident."

In emergency, Luis Fernando was examined by Dr. Luis P., who reports that

> the wound was in the palmar part of the wrist from the thenar aspect to the ulnar side about an inch below the wrist crease. It was very deep; a thick triangular piece of glass was embedded in it, piercing right through to the dorsal surface. . . . A simple glance revealed a cross section of all the palmar tendons, and the radius and ulna were exposed. Radial and ulnar sensation remained, without impairment of circulation. Sensation was absent in the median nerve. X-ray showed no fractures.

After this preliminary examination Luis Fernando was taken directly to the operating room; under general anesthetic the damage was repaired in a difficult three-hour operation. Here is the surgeon's description: "When the wound was cleaned, a complete section of tendons, radials, superficial and deep flexors, and the median nerve were visible. Restoration of continuity of the severed tendons and median nerve was accomplished with the aid of optical magnification. When the wound was closed, the hand was tightly bandaged."

This technical language indicates that the hand had to be sewn back onto the arm, as it was held in place only by the articular ligaments. Fortunately, the radial and ulnar nerves and blood vessels had not been affected; but the median nerve and muscle tendons had been severed. Although the operation was successful, there was concern about restoration of movement and feeling in the thumb and first two fingers. The surgeon warned the parents of possibly permanent loss of sensation as a result of the damage to the median nerve, and of diminished movement because of the severed tendons. He added that their son might need additional operations. In the meantime the wrist would have to be kept motionless, first by means of a tightly wrapped bandage and, after a few days, by being placed in a cast.

A few hours after the operation

As Luis Fernando was coming out of the anaesthetic, he heard the doctor say that his hand was likely to remain immobile, that it would almost be like having an artificial hand, with little prospect of it ever improving. Shortly after leaving the operating room, one of the physicians came to see if he could move the affected fingers, but there was no sensation in the thumb, index, and middle fingers or in the medial side of the ring finger—the area served by the median nerve .

What most concerned the doctors was functional recovery of that nerve. Medical experience shows that after neurorraphy of the median (suture of the two cut ends of a nerve), it takes several months to recover the functioning of the sensory nerve bundle. But the next morning, the doctors were astonished to discover that Luis Fernando was already able to move his fingers and to feel sensation in them. One doctor "laughed incredulously," he recalls, "saying he would like to examine my hand." Then, upon confirming the movement, he added: "Tell me, to whom have you been praying? Who has worked this powerful miracle for you? I operated on you, so I know what was done and what condition your hand was in after the operation."

In fact, the movement and feeling had already begun to return the night before, only a few hours after the operation. That evening the Principal and Assistant Principal of Intisana had gone to visit Luis Fernando in their eagerness to find out how successful the operation had been. When the Assistant Principal asked him if he had been praying for a cure, Luis Fernando replied that he hadn't thought of it, having recovered consciousness such a short time before they came to see him.

> He told me he was going to pray to Blessed Josemaría and gave me a prayer card; I took it with my left hand, but as it brushed my right hand I felt a pricking sensation and said

in a loud voice, almost shouting, "I can feel my fingers, I can feel them!" because previously I couldn't feel them, and it felt something like an electric shock. From that very moment, the movement and feeling started to return. I consider this to be a miracle.

The news spread quickly through the hospital, and other doctors came to see Luis Fernando. "They all stared at my hand, amazed at the way it had recovered from such a serious injury."

After five days in the hospital, Luis Fernando went home with his arm in a cast. After the cast was removed some days later, he started physiotherapy, with excellent results. The surgeon who performed the operation reports: "He has no disability; no further operation is necessary."

A specialist consulted by the Postulation examined the case record carefully and came to this conclusion: "In my judgment, this accident had caused severe damage (traumatic section of the median nerve and the flexor tendons of the hand). Treatment was rapid and correct, with optimum results. Even so, however, clinical experience shows that full recovery from this type of lesion is very rare. What happened in Luis Fernando's case I consider to be well beyond normal expectations."

14. The "Impossible" Josemaría

"Normal delivery in a case of serious Rh (Rhesus) incompatibility." (March 1993)[20]

In November 1993, Bishop Alvaro del Portillo was making a pastoral journey to Andalucía in Spain. On the 20th, he met with several thousand faithful of the Prelature, cooperators and others who were taking part in the apostolates of Opus Dei. In spite of the large number, the gathering had an informal, family atmosphere. It took place in Pozoalbero, a conference center near Jérez de la Frontera.

In the course of this meeting, a mother carrying her newborn spoke up. She was a teacher in Puerta de Santa Maria, a small town near Cádiz. The following conversation ensued between Bishop del Portillo and this mother, who, incidentally, was not a member of Opus Dei.

"Father, I am the second of eleven children, and my father is sitting there beside you. Our whole family would be really pleased if you could give him a big hug, because that way you would be hugging the whole family."

"There, I've done it."

"Thank you, Father. I have four children myself, and I'd like to tell you about a miracle that our Father[21] performed for me. In my third pregnancy there was a high risk for the baby as well as for me. I got pregnant again but had a miscarriage. The sensitization of my blood had increased so much that the doctors forbade me to have any more children. I left everything in God's hands, and within a few months I was pregnant again. From the first moment I knew that this child was coming directly from God, and from then on I entrusted him to the Virgin Mary and to our Father. After a whole series of tests the doctors agreed that the sensitization had disappeared—something scientifically impossible. At twelve weeks, however, there was a

[20] The details of this case are documented in *De fama signorum post beatificationem*, vol. 1, pp. 533–624.

[21] This is the familiar name the faithful of Opus Dei, and many other people who pray through his intercession, give to Blessed Josemaría Escrivá.

serious threat that I would miscarry; again I put myself in our Father's hands. I laid his prayer card on my abdomen with his picture facing the baby. I begged him to save the baby, in the words, 'Save him for whatever purpose you want most. I'll call him Josemaría, and you can send him off to Zaire, or wherever you want! Just let me have him now.' "

"Well done, well done."

"Happily, in spite of more problems, the baby was born healthy, and my blood went back to normal. And here he is, Father," she concluded, lifting up the baby in her arms.

"Thank God, thank God," replied Bishop del Portillo, "I'll bless him with all my love."

"He's called Josemaría."

"Very good."

"I wanted to ask you to bless him because I'm sure that one day God will accept the offering I made of him. And now, Father, my question: What would you say to those mothers who are afraid to have children, and to those who do have them, but then put obstacles in their way when they want to dedicate themselves to God?"

"My daughter, I ask God to enlighten their minds, because motherhood is a very beautiful thing. Responsible motherhood, like responsible fatherhood, means accepting the children God sends and forming them well. To avoid having children is not parenthood at all. Anyway, let's go on. You're so far away that I can't see the baby, but I'd like to give him a kiss. And at the end, if you can bring him to me I'll kiss him. And I'll bless him now, 'in the name of the Father and of the Son and of the Holy Spirit. Amen.' Be calm, carry on, carry on. With your husband thank God for the faith he's given you, that faith which makes mountains melt away like wax. That's how it is with difficulties. When we act with faith, they disappear because the Lord is stronger than we are and he is a Father, a Father who is infinitely good."

Rh incompatibility between mother and child

This case concerns Valentina F. She was thirty-four when she received the favor of the safe birth of her fourth child, through

Blessed Josemaría's intercession. Ten years earlier, she had married Emilio F., a teacher in the same school. They were happily married, both having been brought up in the Faith, and looked forward to having a large family if this was God's will.

A shadow came over these hopes when Emilio was found to have Rh positive blood while Valentina was Rh negative. The resulting incompatibility of their blood meant the possibility of serious consequences for pregnancy and childbirth. Before relating the story, it will be useful to give a brief medical explanation of this incompatibility.

When someone contracts an infectious disease, the immune system produces proteins (antibodies), which have the task of destroying the germs (antigens) that caused the infection. This reaction, common to all organisms, is the basis of the vaccine treatment. The injection of a minute amount of antigen provokes the formation of antibodies, which resist subsequent infection by these germs. Thanks to mass vaccination programs, it has been possible to prevent a large number of infections to the point where some, like smallpox, have been eliminated.

A similar situation arises in the case of an Rh negative woman, whose child inherits Rh positive blood from the father. When the fetus's red cells make contact with the maternal organism (normally at the moment of birth), the mother's immune system sees them as aggressors, and anti-Rh antibodies are formed. As a result the birth sensitizes the mother to the Rh factor. As this takes place only during birth, there is no risk to the first child. However, in subsequent pregnancies the antibodies formed by the mother pass into the circulation of the child and destroy its red corpuscles. Naturally, the more the mother is sensitized against the Rh factor, the greater the damage to the fetus. In extreme cases the fetus will die in the womb.

In the most serious cases in which the baby lives, an exchange transfusion is required, with complete replacement of the newborn baby's blood. In spite of this measure, major damage can still result.

The only way to prevent haemolytic disease of the newborn

is to desensitize the mother after the birth of an Rh-positive baby. This is done with an injection of a protein that neutralizes Rh antigens that have passed from the blood of the fetus to that of the mother. This procedure is not effective in all cases.

A Coomb's test enables doctors to see if a mother is sensitized to the Rh factor. If repeated several times throughout pregnancy, it indicates how severely the infant is likely to be affected.

An increasingly complicated clinical history

The first two children of Valentina and Emilio were girls, born in 1985 and 1987, and the pregnancies were normal. Immediately after the births, Valentina was vaccinated with anti-D gamma-globulin to prevent sensitization, since both girls were Rh positive. The third pregnancy, however, was problematic. In spite of the earlier vaccinations, Valentina began to show signs of iso-immunization, and the indirect Coomb's test registered positive. In August she gave birth to a boy who had to be hospitalized at once because of a high level of bilirubin in his blood. After three days of treatment the infant was still in danger. The mother, because she had already been sensitized, did not need to be vaccinated.

Emilio was warned of the serious risks to his wife and future children if she were to become pregnant again. But as practicing Catholics, the couple refused even to consider contraceptive methods, choosing instead to put their faith in God. At the beginning of 1992 Valentina became pregnant again. Complications set in after the second week, and a miscarriage resulted. At a hospital in Cádiz a uterine curettage (scraping) was performed. Her sensitization to the Rh antibody had risen to an alarming level, but the couple's faith did not waver, and they resolved to use all supernatural and human means to continue having children. At Valentina's insistence, anti-D gamma globulin was administered for a third time, even though it had been ineffective in her last pregnancy.

At this point, the medical professionals strongly discouraged Emilio and Valentina from attempting to have more children and urged her sterilization, but this advice was vehemently rejected because of the Church's judgment that such a procedure is gravely immoral. They continued to put themselves entirely in God's hands.

The birth of Josemaría

In June 1992, less than three months after the miscarriage, Valentina was pregnant again. Prior to a new Coomb's test to establish the degree of her sensitization to the Rh factor, she entrusted the baby in her womb to the protection of Blessed Josemaría Escrivá, whose beatification had occurred only a few weeks earlier, on May 17, and so informed her physician: "I told the doctor that I was going to ask the [school] children to pray that the results of the test would be negative. He suggested in reply that they pray instead that the baby would be healthy, because a negative result from the test was impossible." Her physician was aware that it is medically impossible for a woman with Valentina's clinical history—strongly immunized against the Rh factor during the previous pregnancies, along with the miscarriage—suddenly to be free of all sensitization. Hence his comment that what the children were praying for was an impossibility.

All the relatives of Emilio and Valentina were also having confident recourse to Blessed Josemaría. One of Valentina's sisters, an advanced medical student, put it this way: "For a long time—long in duration and great in intensity; that's how my memory records it—I had been repeating throughout the day: 'Father, outdo yourself! This thing is impossible. Perform one of your wonders!' "

The prayers prevailed, and contrary to all odds the result of the test was negative, an indication that Valentina's sensitization to the Rh factor had completely disappeared, something inexplicable from the standpoint of medical science. According to one specialist who studied the case history, "Medically, this cannot be explained. It is contrary to the basic principles of immunology. When a person makes antibodies in response to a specific antigen—in this case the antigen is the Rh factor of the red cells—that person, on coming into contact with that antigen, will suffer a major immunological reaction, because whatever increases the concentration of antigen increases the intensity of the rejection." This is precisely what the Coomb's test measures.

The sudden occurrence of a negative result after a history like Valentina's could only have one scientific explanation—an error must have occurred in performing the test; it would therefore have to be repeated. This precisely was how the specialists in this case reacted. "When I called my doctor, who is a calm person," says Valentina, "he let out a gasp of astonishment and said that it was impossible." Valentina's sister, having recently completed medical school and with knowledge of the particulars still fresh in mind, reacted in the same way:

> My first reaction was one of profound sorrow, because I thought that the specimen or the chemicals used in the test must have been faulty or for some other reason had given a false result. I was worried that my sister's hopes would falsely be raised, thinking that the immunization had disappeared. . . . I spoke with her seriously about this, and in view of a probable error urged her not to expect too much. I suggested that the test be repeated by another laboratory having no connection with the previous one. "What seems so natural to you," I added, "has no medical explanation. It's like telling me you've seen a pig flying."

The test was repeated, not once but three times, in Cádiz, Seville, and Barcelona, with the same negative result each time.

Still, God wanted to try Valentina's faith. Everything was proceeding normally when the same symptoms that had preceded her miscarriage began to recur. Another of her sisters was with her at the time and immediately handed her a prayer card of Blessed Josemaría. Valentina says:

> I took it, gazed at his image and placed it on my womb face downward toward the baby. . . . I said to Blessed Josemaría,

"Father, save him for whatever purpose you want most. I am praying to you to do this for me. Just let me have this child. . . ." The pains continued. With my mother and sister I started to say the prayer on the prayer card. After saying it once, I noticed a sudden heating of my abdomen and the contraction stopped; the hemorrhaging, too. From that moment on I ceased to have any more symptoms. The following day I went to see the doctor, who found me and the baby completely normal.

Josemaría was born on March 8, 1993, in a perfectly normal delivery. In spite of the repeatedly negative reading of the Coomb's tests—the last one had been in October—the hospital staff was ready for an exchange transfusion of the baby's blood as soon as he was born. There was, however, no need for it; the newborn's Rh tested positive. The Coomb's test on the mother's blood and on the umbilical cord remained negative.

An inexplicable "parenthesis"

The obstetrician who had been with Valentina throughout her pregnancies read her testimony and agreed with it entirely: "It's true. This was impossible." His statement follows: "There are three facts which make this fifth pregnancy extraordinary: (a) The negative result of the indirect Coomb's test, after the iso-immunization of the third and fourth pregnancies and after the miscarriage and curettage; (b) No reaction against the fetus in a patient who was carrying an Rh-positive fetus; (c) The reappearance of iso-immunization in the following pregnancy. I have to admit that in my long clinical experience *I have never come across a case like this.*"

As if to guarantee that this pregnancy was clearly due to divine intervention invoked through the intercession of Blessed Josemaría, the next pregnancy followed the expected course: The fetus was Rh-positive, and during the pregnancy the Coomb's test was positive. In June 1995 Valentina gave birth to a girl with severe jaundice who required a complete exchange transfusion and intensive care. Valentina, too, required special treatment for severe anemia following the birth.

Evidently, things had returned to "normal." The really "abnormal" thing had been the parenthesis of nine months while she carried Josemaría, when what "couldn't happen" did happen. But nothing is impossible for God.

An expert consulted by the Postulation made a careful study of the record and arrived at this conclusion:

> The mother says that after the satisfactory progress of the pregnancy and the normal birth of her son, Josemaría, she assumed that everything would go well with her sixth pregnancy. She did not see any special reason to petition Blessed Josemaría again or ask for his intercession. In my opinion, this is precisely what confirms the extraordinary nature of the "parenthesis" in her iso-immunization, which cannot be explained scientifically. . . . I would like to dwell on what for me is fundamental regarding this miracle, namely the lapse, interval, parenthesis, or whatever one would like to call it, of the negativization of the anti-Rh antibodies of the mother and therefore in the cord blood of the baby, especially since the baby was Rh-positive."

* * *

Josemaría is a healthy, lively boy, the delight of the whole family. His mother insists that the pregnancy and birth of this son were a "parenthesis" in her difficult pregnancies, attributable without a shadow of doubt to the intercession of Blessed Josemaría Escrivá. "It makes me very sad," she writes, "that the new baby girl had to suffer so much in order to confirm the miracle of Josemaría, who today is a cheerful and intelligent boy, the most sociable of the children, and the joy of the family, as we often say."

15. A Terminal Case

"Recovery in two days from fulminating myocarditis." (May 1993)[22]

Blessed Josemaría Escrivá traveled through much of Latin America between May 22 and August 31, 1974. What brought him to Brazil, Argentina, Chile, Peru, Ecuador, and Venezuela, as well as to other countries in that region and in Europe during the 1970s, was the eagerness of a catechist to strengthen the faith and morality of his own children in Opus Dei and thousands of other people who came to hear him.

Those were the difficult years following the Second Vatican Council, when people all over the world were receiving distorted information about the Council and forming the impression that the Church was changing essential aspects of her teaching. It was to reiterate the perennial truths of the Faith and to reassure Catholics in their practice of it that Blessed Josemaría undertook those exhausting apostolic journeys across half the world.

During his stay in Brazil, Paolo F., sixteen at the time, met the founder of Opus Dei in one of several gatherings of young people and even managed to give him a kiss. As we shall see, that turned out to be a major event in his life.

A rapidly developing illness

By 1993 Paulo was thirty-four years old and enjoying generally good health; at the beginning of May, however, he began to experience a persistent cough and had difficulty breathing (dyspnea) whenever he exerted himself. Not until May 18, when he felt unusually tired and noticed pains in his chest, did he pay much attention to these symptoms. When the work day was over, he went to the clinic at Incor Hospital (Cardiac Institute of Sao Paulo), where an examination suggested that he was suffering from cardiac arrhythmia. Initially, he thought

[22] The details of this case are documented in *De fama signorum post beatificationem*, vol. 1, pp. 385–478.

this might be due to concern about one of his sisters, who had recently undergone surgery.

That same afternoon, when Paulo did not respond to treatment, he was admitted to the hospital. Preliminary examination showed an extremely rapid pulse (140) and very high blood pressure; the cause was diagnosed as acute auricular fibrillation. When Paulo underwent defibrillation, the heartbeat at once returned to normal, but as a result he went into a life-threatening shock. The blood pressure fell rapidly below what the instruments could measure, respiration became depressed, the body turned blue (cyanosis), and his level of consciousness noticeably declined. A tube was inserted into his throat to assist breathing, and everything possible was done to raise the blood pressure.

A diagnosis—cardiogenic shock, i.e., shock caused by acute heart failure—was made without knowing its cause. Subsequent testing on the following day showed that it was due to an infection contracted weeks before. That diagnosis was confirmed by the results of procedures carried out the same day. All the means recommended for treating Paulo's case were employed, but his condition steadily deteriorated. The doctors contemplated a heart transplant or the implantation of an artificial heart.

A desperate option

Paulo's parents had been summoned to the hospital on the previous day. His mother describes what happened after her husband, Serafin, had gone back home to get some rest:

> At 4 P.M. on the 19th, I was called by Dr. K.'s medical team to say that they were considering the possibility of a heart transplant. With me were my sister Maria, her daughter Marisa, and the daughter of a friend, Claudia, who worked in the hospital. I said I would leave it to the doctors, but I would want to have my husband's permission. At once I began to invoke the intercession of Blessed Josemaría Escrivá, repeating an aspiration he often recited: "Lord, whatever you want, I want too." But since I lacked the same

courage as the Servant of God, I added my own aspiration: "But help me to want what you want." I didn't want my son to have a transplant, as I was afraid of the consequences. I just wanted him to get well.

My husband returned at 6 P.M. or a little afterward with two of our friends, Claudia and Teresita. The doctors had drawn up the consent form for the transplant and called us in to inform us of the need for anticoagulant therapy—which was unavailable at that particular hospital. It would need to be brought in either from Einstein Hospital or the Portuguese Charity Hospital. My friends offered to help obtain it, and the doctors began to prepare for the operation.

A couple of minutes later I saw the medical team rush to my son's bedside in the intensive care unit. I ran over to the other side of the bed and asked one of the doctors, whose face was as white as a sheet, "Is he dead?" The doctor, who didn't know who I was, replied, "Not quite, but very nearly." As I turned around, I saw the medical team with my husband, informing him that a transplant was no longer possible because our son had suffered liver failure and the failure of other organs as well. All we could do was hope for the best. Would Paulo ever recover? Everything indicated that he would not last through the night. We were permitted to remain in the hospital until 11:30 P.M.

As this testimony indicates, Paulo's condition had dramatically worsened. The heart failure, originally caused by myocarditis, had led in turn to the failure of other organs. First, kidney failure and subsequent anuria (absence of urine); then liver failure; followed by a drop in blood values related to clotting—a precursor to disseminated intravascular coagulation. The gravity of the situation is apparent from a review of the medical literature; mortality in cases of multiorgan failure where more than three organs are affected is 80 percent if the condition lasts longer than twenty-four hours, and rises to 100 percent when it lasts more than four days. Even where the patient recovers, it takes a long time and usually leaves the organs impaired.

Paulo's condition had passed from critical to terminal when a transplant was no longer possible; death seemed imminent. The case notes of his attending physician explain: "I left the hospital that night convinced that he would be dead by the next day. I so informed the family and urged them to go home." Paulo's mother adds: "We did go home, crying, and abandoned everything into God's hands." Her friend Claudia describes the scene: "Those were hours of complete desperation; all we could do was ask for a miracle. . . . I remember remarking, too, that miracles don't happen to people like us."

"Father, give him back that kiss"

As the news of Paulo's condition spread, relatives and friends joined in the prayers for a cure. Several who were in touch with Opus Dei's apostolic work in Sao Paulo turned to Blessed Josemaría's intercession, some of them reciting the prayer card and others using their own words. All were praying with a confident faith, certain that God still performs miracles even in our day; as Blessed Josemaría had written: "Yes, this is still the age of miracles; we too could work them if we had faith!" (*The Way*, no. 583). One person placed a prayer card and a Miraculous Medal next to Paulo's head.

His parents prayed with great persistence; at the time they were also visiting one of their daughters in another hospital as she recovered from surgery. Serafin remained at his son's bedside and did not lose heart when he heard the doctor's final verdict; he continued to ask Blessed Josemaría for a cure. At his request a priest had conferred the Anointing of the Sick the previous night.

In the midst of all this anxiety, Paulo's father suddenly recalled that his son had met Blessed Josemaría in 1974: "At the end of the get-together with young people, when our Father was about to leave, I saw my son give him a kiss. As soon as I remembered it, my prayer for his intercession was simply, 'Give him a kiss and restore him to health.' "

The crisis passed, and Paulo's condition unexpectedly and suddenly improved. "We arrived at the hospital at 6.30 A.M.," his mother recalls, "to hear the news that Paulo's body had miraculously reacted, that there was no need for a transplant, and that we would have to wait and see what happened from then on." Inexplicably—he had been expected to die during the night—the kidneys had started to function, the blood pressure began to rise, and the clotting system improved. The multiorgan failure was apparently correcting itself. Two days later the tube was removed, and Paulo was able to breathe on his own. After another week he was able to leave the coronary intensive care unit and begin convalescence elsewhere in the hospital.

The opinion of the specialists

After Paulo's recovery, one of his doctors wrote:

> As the doctor who looked after the patient throughout the illness, I consider this to be an exceptional case with a highly unusual outcome. I have never seen anything like it during my twelve years of experience as a cardiologist in a hospital dealing with many and varied cases of heart disease. To sum it up, this patient had reached such a serious state that his death was confidently expected, and yet within a few days he had fully recovered; what is also uncommon, there were no aftereffects from that moment on. . . . Recovery was so unusual that it became the subject of an anatomical-clinical meeting in this hospital on November 24, 1993, the proceedings of which were published in the *Brazilian Archives of Cardiology* in May 1994."

Several cardiologists studied the case in an effort to discover a natural explanation for its happy outcome. One of them, a distinguished specialist in a Madrid hospital, reported: "In this case the likelihood of death was very great. In my opinion the patient was correctly treated and managed, and the outcome was favorable, ending in complete recovery. However, from my experience as a specialist in intensive care, I have to say that the favorable outcome of this case was really surprising and remarkable." For him, the extraordinary thing was not so much the cure as the astonishing way in which it happened.

A specialist in Rome gave similar testimony:

> I think the facts are sufficient to establish that the clinical shock reached the phase of irreversibility or very close to it—i.e., a state of coma with respiratory insufficiency, anuria, hepatic necrosis with consistently raised enzymes and coagulopathy. Besides, given the seriousness and rapid progress of the myocarditis, permanent damage would be expected. However, six months after the attack, tests showed an absolutely normal heart, structurally and functionally. I share the astonishment of colleagues who were directly involved in this case; there would seem to be no explanation, despite an extensive search through current scientific knowledge.

The positive and rapid recovery from fulminating (sudden and violent) myocarditis, with the prognosis of death, is clearly due to a grace obtained through the intercession of Blessed Josemaría, who throughout his life was a very grateful person and continues to be so in heaven. In 1974, during his brief stay in Brazil, a sixteen-year-old lad had given him a kiss; he returned it in May 1993, a year after his beatification, when he obtained from our Lord this complete and unexpected cure of a serious illness. "Just like the doctor," says Paulo's father, "I am certain that here we have a miracle. I see it as a 'kiss' from our Father attributable to all the petitions and prayers of friends and relatives."

Claudia, the friend of Paulo's mother, used a phrase in her testimony that provides a fitting conclusion to this story. In that moment of despair, she had remarked that miracles only happen "to others" and never "to people like us." Now, she explains, "Five years have passed, and whenever I see Paulo at the athletic club where he practices gymnastics or some other sport, I look at him and feel happy in knowing that miracles do happen, even to us."

16. In the Space of One Night

"Instantaneous recovery from paralysis of the radial nerve." (February 1994)[23]

Christopher Columbus discovered an island we know as Puerto Rico on November 19, 1493, during his second voyage to America. The mountainous silhouette and bright green vegetation attracted his attention so forcefully that he described it in one of his letters. He took possession of the Island—Borinquen, as it was called by the inhabitants—and named it after St. John the Baptist. When Juan Ponce de León established its capital in 1508, he called it Puerto Rico. Later, in one of the caprices of history, the island and the capital exchanged names.

Puerto Ricans call their land the Enchanted Island, or simply *the Island*. It well deserves this name, for Puerto Rico's location in the Caribbean, as the middle link in a chain of islands that runs from the Florida peninsula to Venezuela, gives it many natural advantages, including the constant northeast breeze of the trade winds and the most agreeable climate in the region. The average annual temperature on the north coast, for example, is 79 degrees, and it varies only slightly from month to month the year round. A gentle climate with abundant moisture and many waterways helps to explain why Puerto Rico is renowned for the quality of its tobacco, coffee, and sugar. A recent upsurge of industry and technology has enhanced urban development. For the large number of tourists, too, Puerto Rico is an enchanted island.

This is the setting in which another extraordinary grace was obtained through the intercession of Blessed Josemaría Escrivá. Before relating the story, it is well to point out what may seem an irrelevant detail: Puerto Rico is the last place where Opus Dei's apostolate began during the founder's lifetime. The first members arrived in San Juan on June 17, 1969,

[23] The facts of this case are documented in *De fama signorum post beatificationem*, vol. 1, pp. 481–530.

after receiving his encouragement and blessing. That makes "the Island" Blessed Josemaría's youngest child.

Pearl of the South

Early growth of the apostolate in San Juan made it possible by 1983 to set up additional residences outside the capital, and first in Ponce, which is known to its citizens as "Pearl of the South" because of its location on the south coast. In that year Guajiles Residence opened its doors to university students from all parts of the island and began to provide them with the same family atmosphere of study and piety one finds in every residence of Opus Dei.

The story begins in August 1993 and concerns Alberto, a twenty-four-year-old resident of Guajiles, known for his athletic ability. On August 1, along with several other residents, he was injured in an auto accident. At the hospital, X-rays showed a comminuted fracture (numerous small fragments) of the left humerus, which caused Alberto to lose the feeling in his arm due to partial paralysis of the forearm and almost complete paralysis of the hand. It was suspected that there was damage to the radial nerve, which controls hand movements.

A provisional splint held the arm in place for two weeks and was then replaced by a cast for six more weeks, the usual length of time required to set this kind of fracture. When it was removed, paralysis persisted in the wrist, with consequent loss of hand movement—a clear indication of injury to the radial nerve. Alberto also suffered severe pain, especially when he attempted to move his hand, and there was extensive inflammation of both hand and wrist.

After another six months without improvement, Alberto was examined in the department of physical medicine and rehabilitation at Damas Hospital in Ponce to determine the degree of paralysis so that appropriate treatment could be prescribed. A test was performed to determine the degree of functionality in the motor nerves.

The clinical report written after the test said that Alberto was unlikely to recover the use of his hand. In the medical literature, about 10 percent of closed fractures of the humerus produce radial paralysis. Of these, the vast majority (90 percent) are functional disturbances and consequently heal spontaneously, even without treatment, in the space of three to six months. In the remaining 10 percent the paralysis is lasting, due to Wallerian degeneration of the nerve; that is, physical destruction of the nerve fibers. Prognosis is poor because clinical experience shows a very slow process of recuperation. In young persons receiving good rehabilitation, the paralysis can be expected to persist throughout their lives.

An operation was conducted on November 24, 1993, in the hope that the paralysis might be merely functional, or possibly caused by compression of the nerve. It revealed instead that the radial nerve was confined within a bony callus that had formed around the fracture and that, in the original accident, a fragment of bone had pierced and injured the nerve. The surgeon was able to free the nerve from that growth and to extract the bone splinter. There was, however, no improvement in Alberto's situation; he continued to experience pain and still could not move his left hand. A splint was applied to prevent the hand from drooping and to encourage its slow recovery; postoperative therapy would at least permit wrist movement.

Alberto summarizes the result of another test taken on the nerve two months later, on Febuary 2, 1994: "The physiotherapist examined me once more by means of electrical stimulation, and confirmed that the nerve was seriously damaged; this meant that I would not recover the movement of my hand." Until that moment, it had not occurred to Alberto to pray for his cure, perhaps because of his confidence in the resources of medicine. Now he began to be seriously concerned at the thought of total and permanent loss of one hand.

A fruitful novena

In January 1994, the chaplain of Guajiles, who had also been in the accident, travelled to Rome. Alberto's name came up while he was speaking with Bishop Alvaro del Portillo, the Prelate of Opus Dei, who assured him of his prayers and gave him a prayer card with a relic of Blessed Josemaría to pass along to

Alberto, with encouragement to place his faith in the founder's intercession.

About halfway through February, Alberto began to say the prayer and continued it for nine or ten days, at the same time placing the relic every night on the scar left by the operation. On waking up one morning, he found that normal movement had returned to his left hand. Here is his account: "A priest of the Work, a friend of mine, was in Rome for a few days and brought back a prayer card of Blessed Josemaría with a relic *ex indumentis* (a fragment of clothing). Immediately, I started to say the prayer, and one night, while I was asleep, I felt discomfort in my hand; due to my sleepiness, I did not take much notice of it. The following morning I tried to move my hand and, unbelievably, it responded. Evidently the radial nerve had recovered, for I was able to make all the movements the neurosurgeon had recommended."

It is easy to imagine the surprise of Alberto's fellow residents when he greeted them that morning without the splint he had been using to support his hand and demonstrated his ability to perform all the movements that he had been unable to do before. But the major surprise was registered by the medical professionals, given that the complete cure of organically caused paralysis (physical destruction of part of the nerve) is inexplicable without some preceding sign of functional recuperation.

A few days before the sudden cure, the director of physical medicine and rehabilitation had made a new examination and issued the following prognosis: "My opinion, based on clinical data, both electrodiagnostic and scientific, is that this unfortunate young man will continue to have significant (40 percent) dysfunction of the superior left extremity and a total incapacity of 25 percent according to the 'Guidelines for Evaluation of Permanent Incapacity.' This will make it difficult for him to carry out manual operations which require strength and dexterity and put an end to participation in the sports he had previously practiced."

Here is Alberto's description of that doctor's reaction when presented with evidence of his cure: "When I went to the hospital and the physiotherapist saw the movements I was able to perform with my hand, he said he had to accept that it was a miracle. I am certain that this favor was granted through Blessed Josemaría."

* * *

Four years later, Alberto is able to perform all the normal movements with both his hand and arm, and he takes part in all sports without the least impediment.

17. Three Months to Live

"Surprising cure of a serious pancreatic illness." (December 1996)[24]

Rosa L., a married woman with two children, was living in Rome. She had had two major operations: a hysterectomy in 1990 and an operation to remove breast cancer in 1994. Because of this medical history she used to go for regular, thorough, medical check-ups. Each time, the results were normal, until May 1996, when the illness from which she was surprisingly cured was first detected.

The first indication was acute abdominal pains. A gastroscopy revealed a small ulcerous lesion in the duodenum that was in the process of healing and could not have been causing the pain. After another examination in June, these were the symptoms: "A band of pain in the epigastric region radiating towards the back, unrelated to meals and not affected by treatment with Ranitidine or Omeprazol." Something other than an ulcer was responsible, but at this point the only treatment was to relieve the symptoms of non-specified digestive pains. A new analysis in August disclosed increased anemia, with a concomitant increase in platelets. The white cell count was normal, as were the main blood parameters. Certain electrolytes showed lower than normal figures.

Four months of progressive deterioration

By early September, along with the persistent symptoms, the general state of Rosa's health was rapidly deteriorating, as evidenced by an alarming loss of weight. Her physician decided upon a CAT scan in an effort to identify the underlying cause. The scan revealed an irregular growth in the head of the pancreas, and in the region of the gastro-oesphagal junction, extending along the lesser curvature of the stomach; small nodules were present, and contrast coloring helped to identify these as metastatic lymphadenopathy. These second-

[24] The facts of this case are documented in *De fama signorum post beatificationem*, vol. 1, pp. 661–886.

ary cancers were evidently originating from a cancerous tumor, probably in the pancreas. The scan also showed a large quantity of fluid in the left of the thorax, and more fluid in the pericardium.

All of this meant that Rosa's overall condition was so alarming that the radiologist decided to wait before informing her until he could speak in private with her husband. She was immediately admitted to the hospital. Her weight was down to 103 pounds. A thoracocentesis (insertion of a needle through the thoracic wall) was performed and a great deal of fluid extracted from the pleura, most of it blood with a high number of white cells and no evidence of cancerous cells.

After diagnosing cancer of the head of the pancreas, Rosa's physicians consulted several oncologists, who agreed with that judgment. It was not considered necessary to carry out a biopsy of the tumor, since the evidence was sufficient and a biopsy might spread the tumor further. It was decided to treat Rosa with Gemcitabine, a new form of chemotherapy; her life expectancy was only three months.

Desperate to use every possible measure to save Rosa's life, her husband Franco consulted a specialist in Milan, who referred him in turn to a Swiss professor with expertise in that type of tumor. Both reaffirmed the diagnosis, but it was not possible to be absolutely certain, absent a histological analysis. Accordingly, Franco decided to carry on with the prescribed treatment, which had already begun. Rosa had received one cycle of the chemotherapy (three applications over one week), and two more cycles were planned, with a break of one week in between. But the general state of her health was deteriorating too rapidly to permit them. Her weight was down to 87 pounds, and an X-ray of the thorax on October 22 showed more large accumulations of fluid in the pleura.

Another analysis one week later showed that the lungs were in critical condition, with still more fluid building up. It was decided to continue treating Rosa with corticosteroids and to begin intravenous feeding in her home. A new CAT on November 18 showed nodules at the base of the right lung; these, as the radiologist reported, were "consistent with metastases."

The scan also showed a round mass in the head of the pancreas with a maximum diameter of one and a half inches; its density seemed to be that of fluid. A similar image showed up at the base of the pancreas.

On November 22, more fluid was drawn from the pleural cavity, most of it blood. Blood tests showed severe anemia, and the white corpuscle count varied. Antibiotics were administered orally to combat infection. In mid-December, with the symptoms continuing, antibiotics were given by intramuscular injection, together with pancreatic enzymes. A crisis seemed imminent.

Invocation of Blessed Josemaría

During those months of suffering, Franco was supported by friends, including several members of Opus Dei who lived in Rome. "My friend Andrés," he writes, "was one of the first people to hear of my wife's illness. . . . On September 19, he sent me the following note: 'Dear Franco, I'm praying for your wife's cure through the intercession of Blessed Josemaría. This relic may help you to pray. Be sure to pray with lots of faith!' " Franco was grateful for the relic *ex indumentis* of Blessed Josemaría, which he placed on his wife's bedside table. Holy Mass was offered for her recovery in the crypt of the prelatic church of Our Lady of Peace; Blessed Josemaría's body rests just above it under the main altar. "I received solidarity and affection from all sides," Franco's account goes on, "but the doctors were giving us very little hope that she would live, and my faith in divine things was not strong enough for me to hope for a miracle."

Rosa's condition had continued to deteriorate when suddenly, toward the end of December, she began to improve. Franco recalls the exact moment when the change occurred: "A few days before Christmas my wife asked for Holy Communion. Our parish priest came . . . and she did receive. From that moment there was rapid and continuous improvement, as confirmed by analyses and scans." When she gained several pounds within a few days, doctors decided to hold off on further treatment. On January 15, another total body scan showed notable improvement in the clinical indications, both in the lungs and the pancreas. A nodular mass less than an inch in diameter was still apparent in the pancreas. By March 4, lung X-rays were almost normal; on that same day an ultrasound scan showed that the pancreas was somewhat atrophied, but there was no trace of the nodular mass. Laboratory analyses also showed noticeable improvements.

Franco gave the news of Rosa's extraordinary and unexpected cure to the priest of Opus Dei who had celebrated the Mass near Blessed Josemaría's tomb: "Your prayers . . . and Blessed Josemaría's intercession have worked a miracle! My wife—and you saw the state she was in—has been cured of the disease the doctors had called 'incurable.' I wish I had as much faith as you have, to be able to appreciate to the full what a great gift God has given me. I thank you with all my heart."

A cure without medical explanation

The Postulation asked several doctors to make a clinical study of this case. After reviewing the foregoing data, they concluded that Rosa's illness must have been either a cancer of the pancreas or acute pancreatitis—which of these it was impossible to determine scientifically in the absence of a biopsy of the tumorous mass in the head of the pancreas. Taking into account the patient's symptoms, the experts inclined to the opinion that it must have been acute pancreatitis, erroneously diagnosed and treated as cancer.

After carefully studying the record, a radiologist observed that "radiology of the pancreas is a somewhat difficult field of study, as it is often impossible to reach a judgment with absolute certainty. Moreover," he added, "my study was carried out *a posteriori*, meaning that I had all the clinical data at my disposal after the case history was already competed." Hence his conclusion:

> In the absence of histological tests, the possibility of a cancerous tumor cannot be definitely excluded. But radiologically, the clinical manifestations seem to be those of pancreatitis. One must add, however, that this was a very

serious form of pancreatitis, which makes the outcome extremely surprising. Even if it had been properly treated, complete disappearance . . . of the pulmonary lesions and the state of the pancreas at the end of the illness would still have been something quite outside normal clinical experience.

The intern who carried out the final case review, after making a detailed differential diagnosis between the most probable hypotheses (pancreatitis; pancreatic cancer; metastasis of the earlier breast cancer), concluded that Rosa had suffered from pancreatitis, undiagnosed and therefore untreated. His words are noteworthy: "It must be said that the patient's complete recovery is something extraordinary, whatever the diagnosis. If it was cancer of the pancreas, which is one of the most aggressive types, such a cure has no explanation in the present state of medical science. If it was pancreatitis, it must have been a very serious form of it, and without the correct treatment from the beginning or the application of any of the usual remedies, her recovery is absolutely astonishing. The remedies that were applied were minimal, given the seriousness of the case, and the sudden gain in weight and improvement in the general state of health in such a short time are likewise very striking. If acute pancreatitis had been diagnosed, the patient would very probably have been confined to the intensive care unit," not treated at home.

Franco put it more simply on June 30, 1997: "At the present time, following the latest analyses and scans (the most recent being on June 25), Rosa seems to have been fully cured from what the specialists had called an 'incurable' illness." The professor who had been carefully monitoring her case told Franco after the last medical examination something he will never forget: "Here we have a miracle."

* * *

Having completely recovered from this illness, Rosa died two years later, at the end of November 1998, after suffering a heart attack (myocardial infarction); according to the medical professionals, it was unrelated to the illness from which she had been cured.

18. A Surgeon's Hands

"Cure of a cancerous chronic radiodermatitis."
(November 1992)[25]

Many cures having no explanation in light of present-day scientific knowledge have been attributed to the founder of Opus Dei since his beatification. Among them the Postulator chose this case for submission to the Congregation for the Causes of Saints. A pontifical decree dated December 20, 2001, recognized the miraculous nature of this cure and opened the way for canonization.

The canonical process that led to this result was conducted in the diocese of Badajoz, Spain, the hometown of the person cured. Following established norms, the Postulator presented to the Bishop of Badajoz on December 30, 1993, the relevant documentation and formally petitioned that the diocesan investigation of the alleged miracle be opened. Nine witnesses were called to present evidence before the tribunal, which sat from May 12 to July 4, 1994. They were: Dr. Manuel Nevado, who received the cure; three physicians who followed the whole development of the disease (a dermatologist, a radiologist, and an anatomic pathologist); a nun who provided Dr. Nevado with nursing assistance in the operating room for many years; his wife, also a nurse, who assisted his surgical work; the person who encouraged Dr. Nevado to seek the intercession of Blessed Josemaría; and two priests who knew Dr. Nevado and could testify to his character and credibility. According to established norms, the tribunal also named two other expert witnesses: a professor of dermatology and a specialist in radiology and oncology.

On July 7, 1994, the minutes of the diocesan proceedings were presented to the Congregation for the Causes of Saints. The Congregation issued the decree of validity on April 26,

[25] The *Positio super miraculo*, documenting this extraordinary cure, appears in a 296-page book, along with the statements of witnesses, medical reports, and all the evidence required to prove the miracle.

1996, thus confirming that the investigation had been carried out in full accord with the juridical norms currently in practice.

The case was then transferred to the Congregation's medical committee, the body charged with the scientific study of alleged cures. After a thorough investigation, which included consultation of all relevant scientific bibliography, the committee unanimously declared, on July 10, 1997, that the cure of this disease was scientifically inexplicable. Here are its exacts words, as they appear in the record: "*Clinical diagnosis*: a severe cancerous state of chronic radiodermatitis in its third and irreversible stage (five votes out of five). *Prognosis*: incurable (five out of five). *Treatment*: None was followed (five out of five). *Mode of cure*: very rapid, complete, lasting, and scientifically inexplicable (five out of five)."

The next step in a cause of this kind is the responsibility of theological consultors, whose role is to pronounce that the cure occurred outside of natural causes and that it resulted from the intercessory prayers on behalf of the person cured. The seven consultors met on January 9, 1998, and unanimously affirmed the miraculous nature of the cure and its attribution to the intercession of Blessed Josemaría Escrivá. A majority of consultors classified it as a second-degree miracle, meaning that it was not only the way the cure took place (*quoad modum*) but also the disappearance of a disease that is in itself incurable (*quoad subiectum*).

The Congregation's norms require that its cardinal and bishop members give their approval before the corresponding pontifical decree is issued. This was carried out at the Congregation's Ordinary Assembly on September 21, 2001.

An occupational disease

The condition from which Dr. Nevado was cured is normally classified as an "occupational disease," meaning that it was contracted in the course of his ordinary work. The term covers a wide range of pathological conditions of varying degrees of seriousness and occurrence, such as silicoses in coal miners, different types of poisoning that can affect workers in chemical industries, cancerous lesions resulting from contamination by radioactive materials, and so on.

A particularly dangerous disease is chronic radiodermatitis, which is typically caused by prolonged overexposure to X-rays in medical doctors lacking adequate protection. Nowadays this is infrequent, but years ago it was not unusual in pediatricians, who would hold children in their arms while observing them under radioscopy. It could also happen to orthopedic surgeons using X-ray equipment to monitor the repair of fractures. Dr. Nevado contracted this disease in the course of his surgical practice over many years.

Manuel Nevado Rey was born in Herrera de Alcántara (Province of Badajoz) in 1932. His parents managed the family farm. They sent him to study medicine at the University of Salamanca; he received his medical degree in 1955. That same year he took a position as specialist in orthopedic surgery at a hospital in Santander. There he met Consuelo Santos, whom he would later marry. Like other orthopedic surgeons at that time, he used an X-ray machine to diagnose and repair fractures. Spanish doctors called the apparatus a "*bola de Siemens*" because of its spherical shape and manufacturer.

The surgeon would place the broken limb between the emitting source and the radioscopic screen, using his hands to press together and align the broken bones. As the definition on the screen was very poor, this required maximum power and a lengthy exposure. The apparatus did not allow for sufficient protection against radiation. While this involved no serious danger for the patient, its repeated use by the surgeon could cause overexposure to Roentgen rays, especially to the left hand, which held the broken limb in front of the source.

The experts who investigated this case made an exhaustive study of the etiology, evolution, and prognosis of radiodermatitis. It results when the skin absorbs large amounts of radiation, which impede normal development of the skin tissue. It is well known that radiation once absorbed cannot be eliminated; its accumulation eventually produces irreversible cellular disorders, which become chronic and progressive.

Only if the exposure ceases when the disease is still in its initial stage can it heal of its own accord.

The disease evolves through three stages. In the first and milder form (simple chronic radiodermatitis), the skin becomes dry, fine, and hairless, due to atrophy of the epidermis, and vulnerable to minor cuts and bruises. There is also discoloring, with areas of increased pigmentation and small spots caused by extravasation of blood; organized hematomae make it look as if stained by coal. The skin becomes scaly, ridges of epidermis that form the fingerprints disappear, and ulceration may occur.

In the second stage (progressive chronic radiodermatitis), warts and ulcers appear and continue to worsen even after exposure to radiation ceases. Hyperkeratotic plaques (thickening of the epidermis) and painful keratoses form on the sides of the fingers and fingertips. Pain caused by the ulceration causes the hands to lose their natural flexibility. Around the edges of the ulcers hyperplasia (malignant warts) may occur, and the skin develops telangiectases (dilatation of the small blood vessels), epidermal atrophy, and fibrosis.

With malignant chronic radiodermatitis, the ulcerous lesions become malignant, giving rise to cancer of the skin, especially squamous cell carcinoma and basal cell carcinoma. These may appear much later, often as many as twenty or thirty years after prolonged radiation exposure. If not removed by surgery, the lesions may metastasize via the lymphatics to local lymph nodes, and ultimately blood-borne metastatics may spread to distant organs, endangering the patient's life.

Treatment is quite complex. First of all, it is imperative to cease exposure to radiation at the onset of the disease, but this may be difficult to do if it means abandoning one's medical practice. Fortunately, at least in developed countries, improved technology and more stringent laws have brought more protection. Where malignant or premalignant lesions have appeared, drastic surgery is recommended to prevent their spread; this can mean amputation of the affected fingers or even of the hand or forearm and dissection of the elbow or axillary lymph nodes, depending on how badly they are affected.

Dr. Felipe Calvo, the expert appointed by the diocesan tribunal and author of an exhaustive study of the medical bibliography available on this disease, reached the following conclusion: "Not a single case can be found of spontaneous remission in patients who have suffered from advanced chronic radiodermatitis produced by prolonged diagnostic radiation, or who have developed an epidermal carcinoma following radiodermatitis."

After thirty years of evolution

Dr. Nevado had worked with the Siemens X-ray tubes from the beginning of his practice. After a year in Santander, he moved to Badajoz to do his military service, was assigned to the Military Hospital, and worked as orderly in the orthopedic department. He continued to use the unprotected X-ray equipment available at the time to repair fractures, extract foreign bodies, and perform other procedures. At the end of his military service, Dr. Nevado joined the traumatology department of a Social Security facility in Badajoz, remaining there until 1962. By then he had been working full time at his profession for more than six years.

In 1962 he was appointed Medical Administrator and head of the department of general surgery and traumatology in Almendralejo, a small town near Badajoz, at a hospital run by the Sisters of Charity of Our Lady of Mercy. He carried out all types of surgical operations and continued to use X-rays, though less frequently. He ceased doing so altogether only in 1982, when he began to work at the Social Security Medical Center in Zafra, another small town near Badajoz.

The first lesions of chronic radiodermatitis appeared in 1962, the year he married. Dr Nevado's wife, a certified surgical nurse, recalls that the back of his fingers on both hands had already become hairless, and the skin showed small plaques of erythema, especially on the middle fingers of his left hand. These lesions corresponded to the first stage described above. Although Dr. Nevado and his wife knew their origin, they did not give them much importance.

As the years passed, these lesions developed second-stage symptoms, such as wider areas of erythema, the appearance of large hyperkeratetic plaques, and warts and ulcers of various sizes. Dr. Nevado felt obliged, however, to continue using radioscopy until 1982. The Postulation asked for a study of the amount of radiation his hands would have absorbed during the many years of his practice. The specialists who conducted that investigation based their calculations on information provided by Dr. Nevado and the other witnesses, taking into account the technical characteristics of the "Siemens Tube." They concluded that between 1955 and 1962, while he was practicing at the Social Security facility in Badajoz, Dr. Nevado would have received each year a dose seven times greater than the present annual allowable maximum for X-ray personnel.

The effects of overexposure became more and more apparent in the following years. From 1982 on, the lesions began to cause sharp pain and acute discomfort when his hands rubbed against anything. The testimony of Sister Carmen Esqueta, a Sister of Charity of Our Lady of Mercy, is especially pertinent, for she worked with him as surgical nurse for many years, first at the hospital in Almendralejo (1962–1967), and after 1982 in Zafra. Over this period of twenty years, she noticed how Dr. Nevado's hands gradually changed, as the symptoms went from skin irritations to loss of feeling in the fingers, eczemas, and, eventually, ulcers. "Eventually," she writes, "it became too painful for him to scrub his hands properly with good detergents using a brush, as all surgeons do before performing operations. Surgeons also put talcum powder on the inside of their gloves. Eventually Dr. Nevado could not even tolerate the talcum powder. He would put on sterilized linen gloves under the rubber ones."

His discomfort became so great that about 1984 or 1985 he had to limit himself to minor surgery requiring less stringent antiseptic measures. Even so, by 1992 he had to abandon even minor procedures, due to the deterioration of his hands. According to Dr. Nevado's wife, who was his surgical nurse for a number of years,

> the decisive period came some months prior to November 1992 when he had to stop operating altogether. For over a year he had experienced increased pigmentation of the skin with ulceration on the back of his hands. Most important, an extensive ulceration occupied the whole of the back of the middle section of his middle finger on the left hand. This was very deep and "indolent." Even before the ulcers appeared, my husband had to use different types of dressings on his hands to perform operations. He was convinced that his condition was irreversible and would lead to the end of his surgical practice.

This thought, of course, had occurred to Dr. Nevado long before, as the lesions to which he had given little imporance grew worse. But as usually happens when physicians themselves face disease, he did not formally consult his colleagues. He spoke casually of his concern with two friends, a dermatologist who examined him a number of times and followed the evolution of his lesions, and a professor of dermatology at the University of Extremadura, who offered to remove the lesions and carry out a skin graft. This specialist had added that, in his opinion, if Dr. Nevado did not have his hands treated, he risked amputation. Dr. Nevado's son, Manuel, a specialist in pathological anatomy, offered the same advice, but it went unheeded.

Dr Isidro Parra, another dermatologist friend who had followed the progression of Dr. Nevado's condition, offered this testimony during the process: "In 1992, on the feast of St. Joseph (March 19), when I looked at his hands, the lesions looked like verrucose tumors. This clearly indicated skin carcinoma. . . . There was not only a suspicion that he might possibly develop an epidermal cancer; the fact is that I was sure he already had one. Although no biopsy was made to confirm such a diagnosis, my clinical experience told me that without doubt it was a malignant tumor."

When all these expert opinions are taken together, along with Dr. Nevado's own testimony, there is agreement that his skin lesions had reached a cancerous state by 1992. The radiodermatitis was in its final stage. By the time his cure took place, Dr. Nevado had resigned himself to the possibly fatal consequences of his condition and made no attempt at treatment. He acknowledged this in the canonical process without elaboration, while admitting a fear that the lesions, if malignant, would metastasize.

The cure

Early in November 1992, Dr. Nevado visited the Ministry of Agriculture in Madrid to inquire about the situation regarding vineyards, following a series of regulatory interventions by the European Community. His family had been cultivating vines for some time, and he was deliberating whether it might be better to grow other crops instead.

As the person in charge of those matters was not immediately available, Dr. Nevado was attended by an agronomist, Luis Eugenio Bernardo. After discussing the matter with him and producing copies of the relevant regulations, Mr. Bernardo noticed his hands and especially his fingers, which were red and "raw." When asked about it, Dr. Nevado replied that the lesions were due to an occupational disease caused by prolonged exposure to X-rays and that the disease was progressive and incurable. He added that for the last five months the condition of his hands had prevented him from performing any operations and that it was causing him much discomfort.

The young agronomist writes: "With the best of intentions and wanting to offer my help, I gave him a prayer card of Blessed Josemaría Escrivá, the founder of Opus Dei. . . . His beatification had taken place just a few months before, and I recommended that he seek his intercession by asking the favor of a cure. He thanked me for the prayer card and for my concern, and we said goodbye after exchanging our visiting cards."

With surprised amusement and gratitude, Dr. Nevado related the incident to his wife but never mentioned it again. He did, however, begin immediately to pray that his hands be healed through the intercession of Blessed Josemaría. "I did this," he says, "from that very moment. A short time later (it must have been toward the end of November or the beginning of December), I traveled to Vienna to attend a medical conference. While there I was very impressed to find prayer cards of Blessed Josemaría in all the churches I visited. This led me to invoke his intercession more often, as I had been asked to do. I prayed in an informal way, commending myself to his intercession, without using the words on the prayer card, though sometimes I did say them."

It had been nearly two weeks after his trip to Madrid on November 12, 1992, when Dr. Nevado went to Vienna. His wife, who accompanied him, also recalls how impressed they were to find prayer cards of Blessed Josemaría in a number of churches, along with some of his writings. "My husband and I," she writes, "were very surprised to find so many prayer cards of Blessed Josemaría in all the churches we visited, and we remarked to each other about how universal the devotion to him had become. I also think we spoke of the little appreciation we had, having him so near us, in contrast with a place to which devotion to him had spread."

Undoubtedly this trip to Vienna increased Dr. Nevado's faith in the intercession of Blessed Josemaría, whom he had begun to invoke only a few days before. Back home from Austria, he continued to ask for the intercession of the founder of Opus Dei, which was already becoming evident: "From the day I was introduced to the prayer card, from the moment I first placed myself under the protection of Blessed Josemaría, my hands began to improve; after approximately two weeks the lesions disappeared, and my hands were perfectly well, as they are now."

A perfect and lasting cure; now back to work

Only close friends had been aware of the gravity of Dr. Nevado's condition. Besides his wife and children, the only others were medical professionals who had examined the lesions and who worked with him in the operating room. He explains: "Not many people noticed them because I did my best to conceal them." And his wife adds: "He did not hide his disease, but neither did he talk about it. No photographs were taken of his hands. Neither did he follow any specific treatment, beyond applying soothing ointments to the skin and antiseptics to the wounds."

In the same way, the news of his cure did not spread further than his small group of confidants. Dr. Nevado's characteristic reticence is illustrated by the following example. One of the nurses who had assisted him in surgery expressed her great surprise that he had been cured when she saw him early in 1993, after he had resumed his practice. "He began to operate again in January," she says, "and as I had been his nurse before, I was so pleased to see him at work; the large ulcers he had suffered from were completely healed, and no visible abnormality remained on the skin of his hands. I have not asked him how he was cured of such a serious disease, which had so long afflicted him."

Dr. Nevado did make one exception—the agronomist who had put the prayer card of Blessed Josemaría into his hands. As they had exchanged visiting cards, he phoned the young man a few days before Christmas 1992. "He wanted to tell me, and with great joy, that the lesions had disappeared completely, and that he attributed the cure to Blessed Josemaría. He said that he was convinced that the cure had no possible medical explanation."

"Over the telephone," his testimony continues,

> Dr. Nevado also said that when he first received the prayer card of Blessed Josemaría, he did not put much faith in it, but that his faith increased because of a trip he made a few days later to Vienna with his wife. There he had attended daily Mass in the Cathedral and other churches and had seen the same prayer cards in different languages. With the realization that devotion to the founder of Opus Dei had so universal an extension came an increase of his faith in Blessed Josemaría. He began to pray for a cure with greater faith, convinced that God would grant him this favor.

That phone call was providential because it led the civil servant, while still unaware of the extraordinary explanation of the cure, to notify the Vice-postulator of Blessed Josemaria's cause in Spain. This was on March 15, 1993. The Vice-postulator then contacted Dr. Nevado directly to receive confirmation of what had taken place. This led to a preliminary study and a year later to the opening of the canonical process in the diocese of Badajoz.

After repeated and thorough examinations, the members of the medical committee of the Congregation for the Causes of Saints unanimously concluded that Dr. Nevado's cure was a true *restitutio ad integrum*. This means that healthy tissue had spontaneously regenerated formerly diseased and cancerous skin. As previously noted, there is no record of such a case in the medical literature.

The cure was so perfect that Dr. Nevado can now brush and wash his fingers normally before operating and use strong disinfectants (such as iodine), as the occasion requires, with no harm or ill effect. Should he accidentally cut himself, the wound scars normally without leaving a trace, as with any healthy person. It has given him great joy to return to the practice of the life work he had been obliged to abandon. According to his wife, "No ill consequences have remained that could impede professional practice, neither scar lesions nor any type of neurological deficiencies—with regard to strength, sensation, movement, etc."

Dr. Manuel Nevado is very grateful to Blessed Josemaría for the great miracle he obtained for him from God. Here is his own interpretation of the cure: "I can see an unquestionable coherence between what happened to me and the spiritual message of Blessed Josemaría. I had barely even heard of him before, but I have since been reading his works and have been especially impressed by their central theme—the sanctifying value of work. I have devoted my whole life to work, doing everything in my power to serve those who suffer. I don't consider my cure as some kind of a reward, but as a responsibility and a call to work harder."

About the author

Msgr. Flavio Capucci was born in 1946. He holds doctorates in philosophy and theology and is a regular contributor to the journal *Studi Cattolici*. His principal book analyzes the theories of the Italian Marxist Antonio Gramsci and their application to ethics and politics.

Msgr. Capucci was ordained to the priesthood in 1974 and subsequently devoted himself to pastoral work, mainly in university settings. In 1978, he was appointed Postulator of causes of canonization of the faithful of the Opus Dei Prelature—among them the founder, Blessed Josemaría Escrivá, and also Montserrat Grases García, Isidoro Zorzano, Eduardo Ortiz de Landázuri, and Ernesto Cofiño. He has also worked on the cause of Alexia González-Barros.

He is editor of *Romana*, a semiannual publication of the Prelature of the Holy Cross and Opus Dei.